THE 787
BOEING'S DREAM SHIP?

IMAGE • BOEING

f you've travelled with a commercial airline on an intercontinental route in the past ten years, you may well have flown on a Boeing 787 Dreamliner.

Since the type's first flight on December 15, 2009, Boeing's production facilities at Everett, Washington, and since July 2012 North Charleston, South Carolina, have built over 1,000 787 aircraft and over 800 orders are still to be fulfilled. In a world dominated by the Airbus A320 Family and the Boeing 737 series with thousands of orders outstanding, the Dreamliner's statistics might seem a little tame.

Today, three of the world's best-known network carriers that operate 787s - British Airways based in the UK, Emirates based in Dubai and Qantas based in Australia – are, like all others, facing the fall-outs of the pandemic, geopolitical uncertainties, rising fuel costs and lots of competition.

*MAIN COVER IMAGE •
PAUL BUCHROEDER/
AIRTEAMIMAGES*

Given its seating capacity, suitability for long-range intercontinental routes and a low operating cost base, airlines like the 787.

Passenger opinion is also favourable, many enjoy the cabin altitude, mood lightning and large windows offered by Boeing's composite-heavy twin-jet. Based on experience, the editor enjoys the experience of flying in a Dreamliner.

That's good news, but the Dreamliner has suffered a series of big-ticket issues during its service career to date. Problems with batteries early on, post-pandemic, international trade wars and more recently sub-standard production quality issues have impacted the programme.

Thankfully, the production problems have not impacted the flight safety of the 787 but as part of its response to the production issues, on February 15, 2022 the Federal Aviation Administration informed Boeing it would continue to perform the final inspections on new Dreamliner aircraft and retain the authority to issue airworthiness certificates for those aircraft. FAA

authority will remain in place until Boeing's quality control and manufacturing processes consistently produce 787s that meet FAA design standards; Boeing has demonstrated a robust plan for the re-work required on many new 787s in storage; and Boeing's delivery processes are stable.

Faced with the post-pandemic downturn in air travel, uncertain international trade conditions and Boeing's troubles across its other commercial aircraft, the 787 situation adds further woe to the company's performance. A further tragic blow was the crash, soon after take-off from Ahmedebad, of Air India Flight 171 on June 12, 2025. This was the first fatal accident involving a Dreamliner since its launch 11 years earlier.

This special publication looks at the development of the Dreamliner 787, outlines the problems that have beset the type and contemplates a period of stability for what is, after all, an excellent aircraft.

Mark Ayton

B787 Dreamliner. Third edition. Previously published 2016 and 2022. Contains amendments
ISBN: 978 1 83632 176 7
Editor, this update: Paul Hamblin
Original editors: Craig West, Barry Woods-Turner, Richard Benedikz
Previous updates: Mark Ayton
Senior editor, specials: Roger Mortimer
Email: roger.mortimer@keypublishing.com
Cover Design: Steve Donovan
Design: Dan Jarman and SJmagic DESIGN SERVICES, India
Advertising Sales Manager: Sam Clark
Email: sam.clark@keypublishing.com
Tel: 01780 755131
Advertising Production: Becky Antoniades
Email: Rebecca.antoniades@keypublishing.com

SUBSCRIPTION/MAIL ORDER
Key Publishing Ltd, PO Box 300,
Stamford, Lincs, PE9 1NA
Tel: 01780 480404
Subscriptions email: subs@keypublishing.com
Mail Order email: orders@keypublishing.com
Website: www.keypublishing.com/shop

PUBLISHING
Group CEO: Adrian Cox
Publisher: Steve O'Hara

Published by
Key Publishing Ltd, PO Box 100,
Stamford, Lincs, PE9 1XQ
Tel: 01780 755131
Website: www.keypublishing.com

PRINTING
Precision Colour Printing Ltd, Haldane,
Halesfield 1, Telford, Shropshire. TF7 4QQ

DISTRIBUTION
Seymour Distribution Ltd, 2 Poultry Avenue,
London, EC1A 9PU
Enquiries Line: 02074 294000.

We are unable to guarantee the bona fides of any of our advertisers. Readers are strongly recommended to take their own precautions before parting with any information or item of value, including, but not limited to money, manuscripts, photographs, or personal information in response to any advertisements within this publication.

contents

38
46
12
20
28
N1020K
LINER

Boeing has been long-associated with pioneering aviation design. Today, despite the challenges of the 737 MAX debacle, it continues to produce some of the world's most popular commercial airliners. **Craig West** chronicles the US manufacturer's remarkable story.

The Boeing Company can trace its origins back to founder William E Boeing, who left Yale University in 1903 to enter the risky but potentially lucrative American northwest timber industry. It was during his time in Washington State that he developed a fascination with the new phenomenon of aviation. After encountering various early biplanes, Bill Boeing elected to produce his own with the simple brief – 'to build a better airplane'.

On July 15, 1916 he incorporated Pacific Aero Products and, under his guidance, the tiny company grew into a huge corporation of related industries.

Building a
Better Airplane

A Benchmark for Quality

The rebranding of the firm to the Boeing Airplane Company in May 1917 came barely a month after the US had declared war on the German Empire. An order for 50 Model C seaplanes from the US Navy was a huge boost for the fledgling company but the end of the Great War in 1918 led to a glut of military surplus airframes flooding the market and plunged the aviation industry into recession.

Around 95% of America's aircraft manufacturers went out of business and

The jet-powered Boeing 707 was the first in the legendary line of '7X7' series airliners.
AIRTEAMIMAGES.COM/ ATI COLLECTION

Boeing resorted to producing furniture to stay afloat.

The founder's refusal to give up on his vision for the future of aviation would eventually be vindicated in massive proportions.

In 1922 Boeing received an order for 200 pursuit planes for the US Army – the company made a profit on the deal and never looked back.

Flushed with success, the firm entered the airmail sector in February 1927 through new affiliate airline, The Boeing Air Transport Company, which flew 25

Boeing Model 40As under contract to the US Postal Service.

Elsewhere, work continued on new aircraft and, the following year, the firm introduced the Model 80 tri-motor. The type could carry 12 passengers and featured a host of innovations such as wall lamps, ventilation and heating, reclining seats, a soundproofed cabin, small buffet and washrooms with hot and cold water. It quickly become known as the 'Pioneer Pullman of the Air' and, although only 16 examples were built, they set a benchmark for quality.

A New Approach

The late 1920s marked a period of consolidation for Boeing, which was renamed United Aircraft and Transport Corporation in February 1929 after acquiring several aviation specialists including Pratt & Whitney, Hamilton Standard Propeller Company and Chance Vought.

On the production side, the company turned its attention to new materials and proposed an all-metal aircraft, a low-wing

Under the guidance of founder William E Boeing, a tiny aircraft manufacturing company grew into a huge corporation of related industries.
ALL PHOTOS BOEING UNLESS STATED

monoplane with a circular fuselage. Commenting at the time, Bill Boeing said: "We must not dismiss any novel idea with the cocksure statement that it can't be done. We are pioneers in a new science and a new industry. Our job is to keep everlastingly at research and experiment, and let no new improvement pass us by." These bold but prophetic words have rung in the ears of generations of Boeing designers ever since.

The result was the Model 200, the world's first all-metal aircraft. Known as the Monomail, the sleek aircraft had an open cockpit, but incorporated three compartments

able to hold up to 2,300lb (1,043kg) of cargo. A second version, the Model 221, took flight on May 6, 1930 and featured a slightly longer fuselage able to accommodate six passengers. This heralded the start of the all-metal transport age.

Barely three years later, the bar was set even higher by the Model 247, the first commercial aircraft to incorporate retractable undercarriage. Although it could carry only ten passengers, the type had the capability to cross the US in just 20 hours with seven fuel stops; leading to a 60-aircraft order – worth an unprecedented US$3.5m – from Boeing Air Transport.

The advancements introduced by the Model 247 were soon standard »

> ## "WE ARE PIONEERS IN A NEW SCIENCE AND A NEW INDUSTRY. OUR JOB IS TO KEEP EVERLAST-INGLY AT RESEARCH AND EXPERIMENT, AND LET NO NEW IMPROVEMENT PASS US BY."
>
> **William E Boeing**, Founder and Chairman

throughout the industry and were used to particularly good effect on the rival Douglas DC-2 and DC-3. Their emergence revolutionised the market – between 1936 and 1939, air travel in the US grew by 500%, with 90% of passengers flying on Douglas aircraft.

However, though United Aircraft was holding its own, changes were afoot. The Air Mail Act of 1934 restored competitive bidding in the sector and dissolved the holding companies that brought together airlines and aircraft manufacturers. This led the firm to be split into three – Boeing Airplane Company, United Airlines and United Aircraft Corporation. Disillusioned with the political and legislative processes that had almost forced the company out of business, Bill Boeing resigned as chairman and sold his shares.

All Change

Under the stewardship of Clairmont L Egtvedt, Boeing began studying larger and more complex aircraft. Engineer Wellwood Beall drew up the design for a four-engined flying boat measuring 106ft (32.3m) long, a 152ft (46.3m) wingspan and capacity for 74 passengers and six crew.

With a range of 3,500 miles (5,632km), the aircraft was pitched at Pan American Airways (Pan Am) and, in October 1936, the carrier placed a US$3m order for six of the newly named Model 314 Clippers. The type entered service in June 1939 and offered an extraordinary level of comfort – it had provisions for sleeping berths, a 15-person dining room and dressing rooms for men and women.

Elsewhere, the overall downturn in Boeing's commercial aircraft fortune was balanced by an upturn in military orders. Though the firm lost a competition for a new long-range bomber – the prototype Model 299 crashed during trials – the US Army Air Corps was so impressed by the type's performance that it ordered 13 examples.

The Boeing Model 200 Monomail was the world's first all-metal aircraft and revolutionised aircraft design and construction.

The aircraft, which became the B-17 Flying Fortress, was eventually acquired in huge numbers and became one of the most iconic aircraft of World War Two.

Boeing applied much of the technology pioneered by the B-17 to a new airliner – the Model 307. Known as the Stratoliner, it was the first commercial transport aircraft to feature a pressurised cabin and, fitted with four turbo-charged Wright G-100 Cyclone engines, it completely outperformed the smaller Douglas designs, flying higher, faster and with a greater payload.

The War Effect

The Model 307 set new standards for speed and comfort but the loss of a prototype during a demonstration to Dutch carrier KLM in March 1939 was a major blow for the project and production stopped after just ten examples.

With sales of the Clipper flying boat also dwindling and, at the time, little prospect of a large order for the B-17, Boeing found itself in serious financial trouble. Rivals Lockheed and Douglas were already working

Like many of its predecessors, the Boeing 377 Stratocruiser was luxuriously appointed.
AIRTEAMIMAGES.COM/ KIERON COLLECTION

Then CEO Bill Allen famously "bet the company" on the jet-powered 367-80, which was rolled out of the Renton factory on May 14, 1954.

The 737 has been in continuous production since 1967 and is the world's best-selling jet airliner. *WIKICOMMONS*

> **THE 367-80 WAS A HUGE RISK AND LED BOEING CEO BILL ALLEN TO FAMOUSLY "BET THE COMPANY" ON THE NEW TYPE**

BELOW • The 767 was instrumental in the development of Extended-range Twin-engine Operational Performance Standards (ETOPS). KEY COLLECTION

on transcontinental airliners – the Constellation and DC-4 respectively – leaving Boeing in desperate need of new orders. It was the conflict in Europe that was to shape events.

As the situation worsened and the likelihood of American involvement in World War Two increased, orders for more B-17s were placed. Rather ironically, such was the urgency that Boeing contracted Douglas and Lockheed to produce the aircraft under licence. Work also started on an even more capable bomber, the B-29, that proved decisive in the Pacific theatre and ultimately brought the war to an end with the dropping of two atomic bombs on Hiroshima and Nagasaki in August 1945.

These military projects were directly responsible for another revolution in aircraft construction – mass production. At its peak Boeing was producing 16 B-17s a day in Seattle, a remarkable feat and one that taught the company much about establishing reliable supply chains and logistical organisation – a common feature today.

The Jet Revolution

With the conflict over, Boeing's military orders dried up and the company was left playing catch-up to the Constellation and DC-4/DC-6. It responded with the Model 377 Stratocruiser, a civilian variant of the C-97 transporter and itself derived from the B-29. Production spanned just 56 airframes but, with the war having spurred the development of some revolutionary new technologies such as swept wings and the jet engine, Boeing was already looking beyond its piston-powered airliner.

These innovations were first utilized on the B-47 Stratojet bomber, which crossed the continental US in less than four hours setting a new speed record of 607.5mph in the process. This, and the eight-engined B-52 Stratofortress that followed soon afterwards, gave Boeing a significant advantage in the development of a commercial jet airliner.

Lagging some way behind Britain and its de Havilland DH106 Comet, the US manufacturer opted for a single design that would meet both military and civilian requirements. Even then, it was a huge risk and led Boeing CEO Bill Allen to famously "bet the company" on the new type. The programme was given the go-ahead in 1952 and, at the cost of US$16m, represented nearly all the profit the company had made since the end of World War Two.

Work started on the pioneering 367-80, nicknamed the 'Dash 80', at the manufacturer's Renton, Seattle, facility in great secrecy. It emerged from the production line on May 15, 1954 and flew for the first time on July 15, changing the face of global air travel.

The US Air Force was the first to commit to the aircraft – which entered service as the KC-135 Stratotanker – while the civilian variant was dubbed »

Even by Boeing's standards, the 747 was enormous. The type revolutionised the global market and opened up air travel to millions of people. KEY-CRAIG WEST

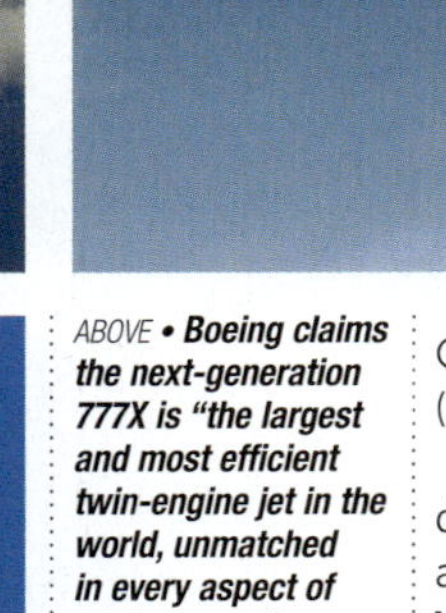

Following two crashes that killed 346 people, Lion Air Flight 610 on October 29, 2018, and Ethiopian Airlines Flight 302 on March 10, 2019, the latest variant of the Boeing 737 – the MAX – was grounded for 22 months.

the 707, the first in a legendary line of '7X7' series airliners. In a remarkable demonstration of the new jet, Boeing test pilot Alvin 'Tex' Johnston flew the Dash 80 prototype over the 1955 Gold Cup hydroplane races on Lake Washington and performed two barrel rolls before the 200,000-strong crowd, which included an incredulous Bill Allen!

Now, seven decades on from those historic events, Boeing has gone on to build an impressive range of airliners. This includes the 727 and 737, which transformed the short- and medium-haul sectors. The latter has been in continuous production since 1967 and, with deliveries now over 10,000, is still the best-selling jetliner in history.

Boeing had forged a reputation for building large, complex aircraft but, even by its own standards, the 747 was massive. At the time of its roll-out in 1966, it was the largest aircraft in the world. The airframe was 225ft (68.5m) long, as tall as a six-storey building and, when pressurised, carried a ton of air. In fact, it was so big that it required the construction of a dedicated 200 million cu ft (5.6 million m³) assembly plant in Everett (the world's biggest building by volume). The remarkable aircraft, which has been produced in several variants including the 747-8 Intercontinental, revolutionised the global market and opened up air travel to millions of people.

More recently, the twin-engined 757 and 767 shifted the focus to operating cost. The aircraft feature nearly identical cockpits, therefore offering a common type rating for pilots, while the latter was instrumental in the development of Extended-range Twin-engine Operational Performance Standards (ETOPS).

The 777 was launched in 1990 and designed to replace older widebody airliners and bridge the capacity gap between the 747 and the 767. It remains the world's largest twin-jet and, with the ability to carry up to 386 passengers in a three-class layout, has transformed the economics of long-haul air travel.

A New Direction

Boeing entered the new millennium facing a difficult choice – how would it build on the success of its '7X7' series airliners and what form would the next-generation airliner take? While European rival Airbus opted for additional capacity in the shape of its double-deck A380, the US manufacturer chose speed.

Launched in March 2001, the twin-engined Sonic Cruiser was intended to fly at up to Mach 0.98, around 15-20% faster than every other airliner in service with the exception of Concorde. Unfortunately for Boeing, it was the wrong aircraft at the wrong time.

Barely six months after the launch of the Sonic Cruiser, the world was rocked by the 9/11 terrorist attacks in the US. This sparked a major global downturn in passenger traffic and, reeling from huge losses, the airline industry was forced to reinvent itself with a renewed focus on fuel efficiency and lower operating costs. This spelled the end for the near-supersonic jet, but the programme was not a complete failure.

Boeing transferred much of the technology it had developed for the Sonic Cruiser to a new concept, the mid-sized '7E7' which, the manufacturer said, promised to deliver "major breakthroughs in a lot of areas starting with the letter E, including efficiency, economics, environmental performance, exceptional comfort and convenience, and e-enabled systems".

The outcome was the 787 Dreamliner, an aircraft that has cemented Boeing's position as one of the world's leading aerospace giants.

> **BOEING HAD FORGED A REPUTATION FOR BUILDING LARGE, COMPLEX AIRCRAFT BUT, EVEN BY ITS OWN STANDARDS, THE 747 WAS MASSIVE.**

The 777X and 787 Dreamliner form the backbone of Boeing's long-haul portfolio.

Dream
Revolution

Barry Woods-Turner reviews the development of one the world's most technologically-advanced airliners to have entered service.

> THE GENESIS OF THE 787 IS BASED ON A PROGRAMME PUBLICLY LAUNCHED BY BOEING ON MARCH 29, 2001, KNOWN THEN AS THE SONIC CRUISER

The Boeing 787 Dreamliner's development has been completely different to any other aircraft programme undertaken by the US manufacturer. Faced with ever-rising labour costs driven by increasing healthcare and pension obligations, the Seattle-based company embarked on its most ambitious risk-sharing venture to date, the likes of which have not been witnessed by the commercial airline industry before. Unlike previous programmes, Boeing sought out both foreign and domestic partners to help spread both the risks and costs

The Dreamliner programme can trace its roots back to the Sonic Cruiser, which was launched by the US manufacturer in March 2001.
ALL PHOTOS BOEING UNLESS STATED

The first public appearance of a 787-8 was given at the 2010 Farnborough International Airshow.
KEY-BARRY WOODS-TURNER

Mount Rainier in Washington State is a stunning backdrop to the sleek lines of the fourth 787-8 prototype, ZA004, N7874 (c/n 40693).

associated with building a completely new revolutionary design. This resulted in a supplier chain involving 43 of the world's leading aerospace contractors, based at more than 130 sites across the globe.

Building a 21st Century Airliner

The genesis of the 787 is based on a programme publicly launched by Boeing on March 29, 2001, known then as the Sonic Cruiser. The jet's sleek design, with a 250ft (76m) long fuselage and a delta wing spanning 164.9ft (50.3m), featured twin tails and canards that would help it achieve high-subsonic cruising speeds up to Mach 0.98. The company said the airliner would carry 200-250 passengers at speeds 15-20% faster than conventional aircraft of the time. The unveiling came shortly after European rival Airbus announced it was proceeding with its double-deck A380 project. Both manufacturers had very different views of how the future market would develop; Boeing opted for speed, while Airbus went for greater capacity.

»

Carrier requirements changed fundamentally after the 9/11 terrorist attack on the US in 2001. The subsequent slump in the numbers of passengers flying resulted in companies rethinking their objectives with efficiency and lower operating costs becoming the most important factor rather than marginal increases in speed. Boeing continued studying the Sonic Cruiser project for another 12 months alongside other more traditional concepts. It finally abandoned the idea in December 2002 as airline interest continued to wane.

The manufacturer remained keen to update its product portfolio and started looking at a new mid-sized, twin-engined aircraft, known as the Super Efficient Airliner and dubbed the '7E7'. The new jet would benefit from much of the research from the cancelled Sonic Cruiser project, including the extensive use of composite materials, the latest bleedless engines technology as well as advanced cockpit and avionics systems. Boeing's stated aim for the 7E7 was to reduce fuel burn by up to 20% compared with the existing generation of widebodies, as well as cutting operating costs by 20-25%.

The company's board gave its approval to offer the 7E7 to potential customers on December 16, 2003. Japanese carrier All Nippon Airways (ANA) was the first to commit the following April, before signing a firm order for 50 examples three months later. The deal was large enough to allow the manufacturer to formally launch the programme. ANA had originally planned to receive it first examples for use on its Tokyo-Beijing rotations in time for the 2008 Summer Olympic Games being held in the Chinese capital, but this was thwarted by production delays.

The Super Efficient Airliner, dubbed the '7E7', was the focus of Boeing's efforts after it cancelled the Sonic Cruiser programme.

ABOVE LEFT • Dreamliners in various stages of build on the initial final assembly line at Everett.

BOTTOM • The first 787-8 to be assembled at Boeing's North Charleston, facility is towed out of the factory in front of a crowd of nearly 7,000 employees and dignitaries.

Development Starts

With the programme given the formal go-ahead, Boeing re-branded the aircraft the 787 in keeping with its well-established '7X7' naming convention.

Initially, the manufacturer planned to offer airline's three variants: the baseline 787-8 seating 242 passengers in a three-class configuration; the 787-3 carrying 290-330 passengers (primarily aimed at the high-density regional operators); and the stretched 787-9 offering 280 seats. The -3 was originally scheduled to follow the -8's entry into service but, lacking customer interest, the variant was initially deferred and then eventually cancelled outright in 2010.

The development of this huge project was beset by manufacturing and technical difficulties, which were further complicated by the sheer number of suppliers and their geographic spread. The first flight test aircraft, N787BA (c/n 40690, ZA001), was rolled-out with much fanfare at Boeing's Everett facility on July 8, 2007 (7/8/07 in US nomenclature) in front of VIPs, airline executives, company employees and the media. It appeared structurally complete and ready to fly but looks can be deceiving.

The manufacturer was, at the time, riding the crest of a wave. The first Dreamliner was built and orders were flooding in. However, like many new high-tech programmes, things can go spectacularly wrong – and they certainly did. The US manufacturer was sure it wouldn't suffer the same fate as its rival Airbus, which was struggling to overcome wiring loom problems associated with its A380 super jumbo. History now shows this confidence was misplaced. Company engineers began discovering faults with some of the manufacturing

Guests excitedly witness the roll-out of Boeing's first 787-8 prototype on July 8, 2007. Few could imagine the problems that lay ahead.

The first 787-8, N787BA (c/n 40690), lifts off from the Everett runway at the start of the type's maiden flight on December 15, 2009, around 29 months after it was first rolled out.

process, leaving Boeing to face one of the biggest challenges in its history.

It claimed structures delivered to the Seattle final assembly line were not finished to an agreed standard. It said suppliers had shipped sub-assemblies that, in some cases, were little more than 50% complete in order to meet the July roll-out deadline. This left Boeing with the huge problem of how to tackle the missing work, made even harder as it had to achieve this on a semi-complete airframe.

Originally, Boeing had thought outsourcing the construction of major sub-assemblies would save time, with fully-fabricated components – complete with all systems, ducting, insulation and wiring in place – arriving at Everett. The final assembly line was ready, with four build positions to speed aircraft through this phase in just 12 days; three days in each position. It had expected to be completing ten Dreamliners a month, an unprecedented rate of production for a widebody airliner. Remedial work took longer than planned, forcing the manufacturer to make several awkward announcements about delays to the programme resulting in the rescheduling of deliveries to customers. More engineering resources were made available in a determined effort to complete work on ZA001.

Detailed discussions with its partners led to the introduction of new quality control procedures. Company engineers were dispatched to provide assistance in improving the standard of components arriving at the final assembly line. There was a marked improvement in the amount of completed work on the second test jet and by the time components for the fourth test example were delivered, at the beginning of July 2008, all the sub-assemblies were supplied complete. Almost a year after its roll-out, Boeing achieved the significant milestone of 'power on' for ZA001, which involved a complex series of tasks and tests that brought electrical power onto the jet for the first time.

Just as the programme appeared to have turned a corner, it was hit by two further blows.

On August 7, 2008 the manufacturer received notification of the first 787 order cancellation – from Azerbaijan Airlines – followed a month later by the walkout of 27,000 members of the International Association of Machinists and Aerospace Workers Union over disagreements about wage increases, healthcare contributions and the company's outsourcing policy. »

> **IT APPEARED STRUCTURALLY COMPLETE AND READY TO FLY. LOOKS CAN BE DECEIVING.**

The strike lasted 58 days and affected all the manufacturer's commercial airliner projects. After workers returned, Boeing reluctantly announced yet another delay to the maiden flight of 787 – its fifth – with the date pushed back to the second quarter of 2009 and service entry moved to early 2010.

On May 3, 2009 ZA001 was finally transferred to the flight line following extensive factory testing. A month later at the Paris Airshow, company officials were confident it would be flying shortly. However, the project was still being dogged by problems and Boeing was forced to announce yet another delay, "due to the need to reinforce an area within the side-of-body section of the aircraft". As the year drew to a close, ZA001 completed high-speed taxi runs on December 12 and the 787 seemed finally set to fly.

Into the Air at Last

Three days later, ZA001 lined-up on the Everett runway. After final checks, and approval from air traffic control, it started its take-off run, lifting into the air at 10:27 Pacific Standard Time (PST). It returned to Boeing Field (from where most of the test flying was performed) three hours later at 13:35. The test programme would involve eight aircraft and was expected to be completed in nine months. By March 24, 2010 the type had been cleared to fly its entire flight envelope.

Early testing proved successful with only minor problems indentified. The third prototype, ZA003, N787BX (c/n 40692), carried out the type's first long-haul, overseas journey when it visited the 2010 Farnborough Airshow, where it was the 'star' of the event. However, testing was suspended following an in-flight fire on board ZA002, N787EX (c/n 40691), on November 9, although the jet landed safely at Laredo International Airport, Texas. The incident was later attributed to foreign object debris in the electrical bay. Testing resumed on December 23, but the company was forced to announce a further delay to deliveries, this time to the third quarter of 2011.

Finally, on August 26, 2011 both the Federal Aviation Administration (FAA) and the European Aviation Safety Agency (EASA) jointly certified the 787-8 at a special ceremony held at Everett. This paved the way for Boeing to deliver the first example, JA801A (c/n 34485), to launch customer ANA on September 25. The jet departed Seattle for Tokyo/Haneda early the following day, arriving in Japan at 09:00 on September 27. The landmark delivery was made some 40 months later than originally scheduled. The airline's second example, JA802A (c/n 34497), was handed over three weeks later and after crew training and familiarisation flights, the type operated its maiden commercial service

TOP • *The first production 787-8, JA801A (c/n 34485), was finally delivered to launch customer All Nippon Airways on September 25, 2011.*

MIDDLE • *Air New Zealand was the launch customer of the stretched 787-9 and took delivery of this special-liveried example, ZK-NZE (c/n 34334), on July 8, 2014.* AIR NEW ZEALAND

ABOVE • *Japan Airlines became the second carrier to put the 787-8 into scheduled service following the delivery of its first two Dreamliners, JA822J (c/n 34832) and JA825J (c/n 34835), on March 26, 2012.*

from Tokyo/Narita to Hong Kong on October 26. This was followed on January 21 by the inaugural long-haul rotation from Haneda to Frankfurt.

By the time of the Dreamliner's next appearance at the Farnborough Airshow in July 2012, the US manufacturer's outlook was a lot more positive. It had overcome a major hurdle and deliveries were taking place with increasing frequency and confidence was rising. This optimism was short-lived as a new set of problems was to besiege the programme.

Battery Fires

Like most new aircraft entering service, the Dreamliner encountered a number of early teething problems including systems failures and other minor incidents. The first few weeks of 2013 were to prove a difficult period for Boeing. On January 7, a battery overheated and started a fire on board an empty 787 Japan Airlines (JAL) example parked at Boston/Logan International Airport. Two days later United Airlines reported a problem with the wiring located in the same area on one of its jets. This led the FAA to announce a comprehensive review of the 787's

critical systems that included the design, manufacturing and assembly processes. A few days later an ANA jet was forced to make an emergency landing at Takamatsu Airport, Kagawa, Japan after the crew received a warning of smoke inside one of the electrical compartments.

This final incident led the FAA to issue an emergency airworthiness directive on January 16 ordering all American-based airlines to ground their 787s, "until yet-to-be-determined modifications were made to the aircraft's electrical system to reduce the risk of the batteries overheating or catching fire". The decision was adopted by other regulatory authorities around the world, effectively grounding all 787s until a solution to the problem could be found. Boeing and FAA engineers investigating the incidents focused on the type's lithium-ion batteries. To get the 787 flying again the manufacturer devised a new battery design which provided three additional, overlapping protection methods to prevent similar incidents. This was accepted by the FAA which published another directive on April 25 detailing the modifications required before flights could resume. The company worked closely with all its customers to ensure the new battery design was incorporated quickly and Dreamliner services were back in the air by the end of the month.

In another incident, a fire started on an empty Ethiopian Airlines 787, ET-AOP (c/n 34744), parked at London/ Heathrow Airport on July 12, 2013 causing extensive damage to the rear of the aircraft. Investigations found the fire was caused by lithium manganese dioxide batteries powering an emergency locator transmitter. The jet was repaired and returned to service on December 23, 2013.

The third variant of the Dreamliner Family is the 787-10.

Expanding the Family

Boeing engineers turned their attention to the second variant of the family, the -9, after the programme settled down and deliveries to customers began to stabilise. The aircraft has a 20ft (6.1m) plug in the fuselage and is capable of carrying 280 passengers in a typical three-class arrangement over routes of up to 7,635nm (14,140km). The manufacturer is building the jet as a replacement for its own 767-400ER and to compete with the Airbus A330.

Pushed by interest from several carriers, including Emirates and Qantas, the company started looking at a further stretch, dubbed the -10. The variant was designed to carry 330 passengers and be a rival for the A350-900, as well as its own 777-200ER. This third 787 variant was launched at the 2013 Paris Airshow with orders and commitments for 102 jets.

Work on the -9 progressed well and the prototype made its maiden flight on September 17, 2013, kicking off a nine-month certification programme.

Notably, Boeing made its first delivery to launch customer Air New Zealand on July 8, a full week before the variant's public debut at the 2014 Farnborough Airshow. The jet, ZK-NZE (c/n 34334), was painted in a distinctive 'all-black' livery and operated the -9's inaugural service between Auckland and Sydney a month later.

Boeing raised production rates as the 787 programme matured. In October 2009, the company selected the North Charleston, South Carolina site for a new 787 Dreamliner final assembly and delivery line to accelerate production faster than any previous widebody programme. The first aircraft rolled out of final assembly on April 27, 2012 and made its first flight on May 23, 2012.

In July 2014, Boeing selected its North Charleston facility to undertake exclusive final assembly of the 787-10. At the time Boeing said the -10's mid-body section produced at the facility was too long to be transported efficiently to its Everett facility. Boeing operates a fleet of four 747-400LCFs purposely modified to transport Dreamlner sections.

On October 1, 2020 the company announced consolidation of all 787 production at North Charleston starting in mid-2021. Boeing said the decision was made to improve operational efficiency in the face of the market downturn brought about by the COVID-19 pandemic.

"THE ADDITION OF A SECOND FINAL ASSEMBLY LINE IN CHARLESTON, SOUTH CAROLINA HAS ENABLED THE MANUFACTURER TO ACCELERATE PRODUCTION FASTER THAN ANY PREVIOUS WIDEBODY PROGRAMME."

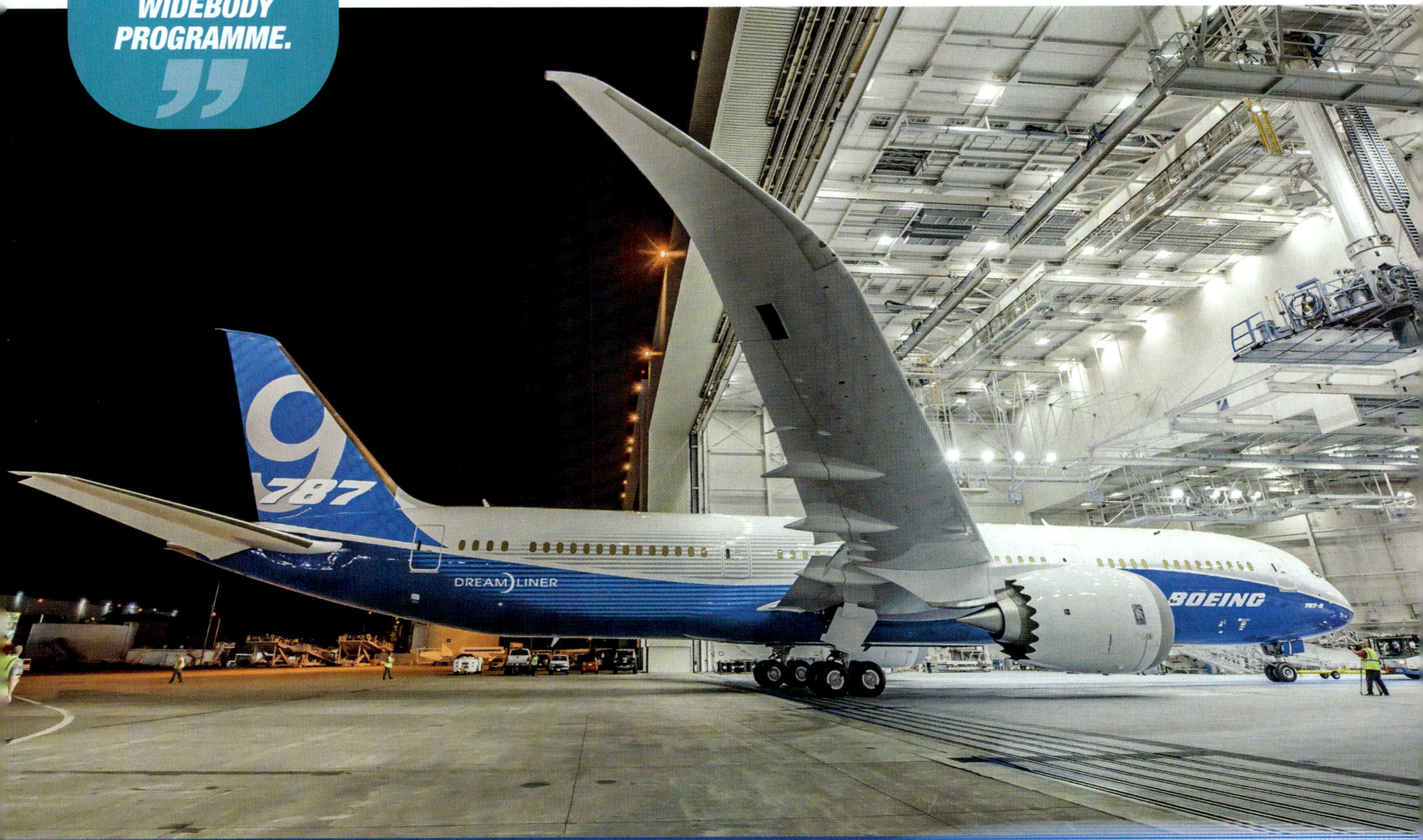

Prototype Boeing 787-9, N789EX (c/n 41988), resplendent in its company livery, is pushed out of the painting facility at Everett. Once the certification programme was completed, the aircraft was delivered to Air New Zealand as ZK-NZD on July 23, 2015.

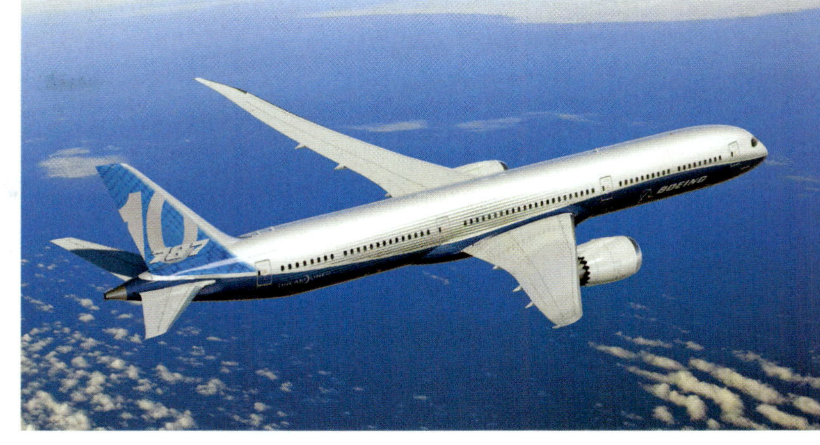

British Airways launched its first Dreamliner service on the London/Heathrow to Toronto route on September 1, 2013. It then added two more North American destinations – Newark, New Jersey and Austin, Texas – before introducing the type to the Indian city of Hyderabad the following March.
AIRTEAMIMAGES.COM/
JONATHAN ZANINGER

KLM Royal Dutch Airlines received its first Boeing 787-9 Dreamliner, PH-HBC (c/n 38760) 'Zonnebloem' (Sunflower), at its Amsterdam/Schiphol base in November 14, 2015. The carrier currently operates 13 787-9s and nine 787-9s.
AIRTEAMIMAGES.COM/
MARTIN BOSCHHUIZEN

LOT Polish Airlines became the first European carrier to receive the Dreamliner when it took delivery of its maiden example on November 14, 2012.
AIRTEAMIMAGES.COM/
DANIEL NICHOLSON

Arke took delivery of three Boeing 787-8s during 2014 and early 2015, but the type didn't remain flying under the airline's name for long. The aircraft were rebranded by parent company TUI on October 1, 2015. *AIRTEAMIMAGES.COM/ RUDI BOIGELOT*

Norwegian established a fleet of 17 787-9 Dreamliners for its low-cost long-haul operation. The Scandinavian carrier withdrew from the long-haul market in 2021. *AIRTEAMIMAGES. COM/ALEX PEAKE*

Thomson Airways became the first UK airline to take delivery of the Boeing 787 when G-TUIA (c/n 34422) arrived at Manchester Airport on May 31, 2013. The carrier rebranded as TUI in 2017 and in 2025 flies a fleet of 13 Dreamliners. *AIRTEAMIMAGES.COM/ SIMON WILLSON*

Virgin Atlantic currently operates 17 787-9 Dreamliners all given female names ranging from Pin Up Girl to Ruby Murray. *AIRTEAMIMAGES.COM/ STEVE FLINT*

Programme **Analysis**

Mark Broadbent analyses the Boeing 787 Dreamliner programme.

BA's first Boeing 787-9 G-ZBKA (c/n 38616) was delivered in September 2015. BA's 787s are powered by Rolls-Royce Trent 1000 engines.

More than ten years after the Boeing 787 entered service on October 26, 2011, the three variants of the Dreamliner are now an established part of airline operations.

The baseline 787-8 entered service with launch operator All Nippon Airways, the longer-range 787-9 was introduced in August 2014 with Air New Zealand and finally, the higher-capacity 787-10 debuted in March 2018 with Singapore Airlines (SIA).

Large network airlines, leisure operators and low-cost long-haul carriers all use the Dreamliner, which also holds the distinction of operating the first regular, scheduled, non-stop flights between the UK and Australia.

It is perhaps an understatement to say the 787 programme's early years did not run smoothly. The aircraft was repeatedly delayed during its development, with the type's introduction to service occurring more than three years later than initially planned.

As a report from Virginia-based aerospace industry analysts the Teal Group reflected: "Management placed entirely too much trust in the design, integration and financial capabilities of its risk-sharing partners. This compounded the problems inherent in a very aggressive up-front programme schedule."

The negative headlines continued after the 787's operational debut. Glitches with the lithium ion (Li-ion) batteries powering the aircraft's electrical system, with incidents in early 2013 involving battery systems on Japan Airlines and All Nippon Airlines 787s, led to a US Federal Aviation Administration (FAA) airworthiness directive (AD) that grounded all 787s for five months that year.

The 787 returned to flight after Boeing developed further safety features for Li-ion battery systems, including an insulator to isolate battery cells from each other and the battery case, more heat-resistant sleeving and wiring inside the battery and a stainless-steel enclosure to isolate the battery unit from the rest of the equipment in the electrical bays. A direct vent to carry battery vapours outside the aircraft was also added.

The 787 has settled down since those troubled early days, the 787's production system matured and toward the end of 2020 the production rate was 14 per month between Boeing's two facilities at Everett, Washington and North Charleston, South Carolina. However, with demand for wide-body jets falling due to the COVID-19 pandemic, on October 1, 2020, Boeing announced that production of the 787 would be consolidated at North Charleston from the middle of 2021 and the monthly rate reduced to five.

Orders and Deliveries

There was a flurry of orders when the 787 was launched and for a few years thereafter as customers rushed to secure delivery slots for an aircraft that Boeing says offers savings of 20% in fuel burn, 30% in maintenance costs and 15% in operating costs compared to earlier-generation aircraft in its size class.

Business plateaued and then fell away in the late 2000s and early 2010s as delivery dates slipped due to the various development delays affecting the programme. From a single-year sales high of 369 aircraft in 2007, the year of the 787-8's roll-out, orders slumped through 2012, recovered to a peak of 109 jets in 2018 before declining in 2019 (82), 2020 (20) and 2021 (-11). The 2018 total was the first year since 2013 that Boeing recorded three-digit annual sales for the aircraft.

Using the 787

With so many Dreamliners now in service, it is worth considering exactly how airlines use the aircraft.

The 787's key advantage for operators is its twin-engine fuel efficiency and range which lets carriers start medium to long-haul route services that would have been unsustainable with older, less efficient equipment.

»

A panoramic view of the 787's flight deck showing the multi-function displays.
AIRTEAMIMAGES

This has led to the most significant impact of the 787: its role in airlines' network development. Boeing says that hundreds of new city-pair connections have been opened using the Dreamliner since the type entered service.

Many of the network airlines who make up the bulk of 787 customers have used Dreamliners to open new services. Most strikingly, Qantas uses 787-9s on a direct Perth–Heathrow service, the first scheduled non-stop air route between Europe and Australia. Meanwhile, North American, and Asian carriers use 787s on non-stops across the Pacific from the US West Coast, and British Airways has used 787s to start new services from Heathrow to secondary destinations with thinner demand, such as Hyderabad, Houston, Montreal, Muscat, and Nashville, among others.

The 787's economics mean the type is useful beyond network development, as it can improve the performance of existing routes in an airline's network by replacing less-efficient older aircraft. SIA told the author that as the airline continues to receive more 787-10s over the coming years, the aircraft will be, "progressively deployed on more and more routes, replacing Airbus A330s and Boeing 777s as they are retired."

Smaller operators, such as TUI, primarily serving leisure markets also benefit similarly from opportunities to operate routes more efficiently. This ability to operate different routes is another of the 787's benefits. All airlines, especially large network carriers, must account for numerous factors (macroeconomics, seasonal travel patterns, competitors' schedules) when planning routes to ensure they put in the correct number of seats to maximise returns.

This means they appreciate an ability to move around capacity to use an appropriately-sized aircraft and help a route run profitably. With the 787-8's 242 seats (two-class) and 7,355nm range, the 787-9's 290 seats and 7,635nm range and the 787-10's 330 seats and 6,430nm range, the Dreamliner variants offer complementary seat and range capabilities while providing single-type commonality.

Independent air transport consultant John Strickland explained: "You don't have the complexity of different aircraft types with different spares holdings. Flight crews can operate across all variants. You can adjust your allocation of aircraft according to different route strengths, and even make some on-the-day, last-minute or ad hoc changes without changing the type or any of the parameters around the operation."

In short, the 787 variants provide different strings in an airline's network planning bow. A 787-8 can be used to try out a route, a 787-9 to fly long range and a 787-10 to add capacity where there is a demand for more seats and revenue cargo.

Many Dreamliner customers operate multiple variants. To choose just a few examples, as of early May 2025 All Nippon Airways was using a mix of 34 787-8s, 44 787-9s and seven 787-10s, American Airlines had 37 787-8s and 22 787-9s, BA 12 787-8s, 18 787-9s and seven 787-10s, Etihad Airways 33 787-9s and ten 787-10s, and LATAM Airlines Chile ten 787-8s and 27 787-9s. United Airlines was the first Dreamliner customer to use all

Boeing's 787-8 is the baseline model which entered service with launch operator All Nippon Airways in October 2011. BOEING

Boeing 787-10 9V-SCA (c/n 60253) arrived in Singapore at the end of its delivery flight on March 28, 2018. Powered by Rolls-Royce Trent 1000 engines, it was the carrier's first Dreamliner.
SINGAPORE AIRLINES

three variants. As of May 2025, it had 12 787-8s, 43 787-9s and 21 787-10s in its fleet.

The 787's Future?

The widebody airliner market might be viewed as one amorphous whole, but there are, in fact, different niches within the niche. The 787-8 sits at the lower end of the market, with around 250 seats, where it competes with the Airbus A330-800. The 787-9 sits in the 250-300 seats area competing with the A330-900 and the 787-10 is in the 300 to 350 seats category competing with the A350-900. The area of 350-plus seats occupied by the A350-1000 and the 777/777X is separate to the categories covered by the 787.

With the 787 variants established in airline operations, Boeing Commercial Airplanes' product development focus has shifted to other projects, principally the 777X, but also the studies into a new mid-market aircraft (NMA), dubbed the 797 by some (although not by Boeing itself), a possible new aircraft in the 'middle of the market' slotting into Boeing's product portfolio beneath the 787-8 and above the 737 MAX variants.

Although big developments with the 787 itself are unlikely in the short term, this doesn't mean activity in the market more widely will not impact on the Dreamliner. The new-generation A330 variants that compete with the 787-8 and 787-9 have sold slowly so far, with the A330-800 having fewer than 20 orders and the A330-900 variant 374 by May, 2025.

This could mean the 787-8 and 787-9 dominate in their respective sectors. The Teal Group says the market has the potential for 3,000 aircraft over 20 years.

As Boeing previously confirmed to the author, its NMA (New Mid-Market Aircraft) studies looked at an aircraft with 220-270 seats and a range of 5,000 nautical miles in terms of seating capacity that's close to the 787-8.

But the 737 MAX debacle and the impact on air transport demand caused by the COVID-19 pandemic had significant negative impacts on Boeing. Consequently, the airframer had its hand forced in delaying the launch of a new airliner, a model that would fill the gap in Boeing's portfolio between the 737 MAX 10 and the 787-8. Additionally, an NMA aircraft would compete with the Airbus A321neo XLR, a model which has sold over 500 jets to date, and the adoption of new technology into its production processes.

787 Systems Evolving

The direction of the widebody market and the ways it will influence the 787 are yet to play out, but in the interim Boeing is not sitting still on the Dreamliner.

Big data has attracted more attention in numerous industries in the last few years. The term, broadly speaking, refers to the gathering of information generated by connected hardware and software and how businesses then use that information to help their operations.

With aircraft, their engines and systems generate huge volumes of data, this is unsurprisingly a pertinent issue in aerospace. In recent years, OEMs have introduced new digital analytics to provide insights into aircraft health, fleet performance and flight operations, and diagnostic/prognostic tools to support maintenance, engineering, supply chains and inventory.

A spokesperson from Boeing's Global Services division told the author: "Newer aircraft are generating a lot more data. Boeing's 787 creates over a terabyte of data during a typical flight. This data generates more opportunities to apply analytics in a way that uncovers greater efficiency and allows proactive approaches in aircraft maintenance operations."

Boeing Commercial Airplanes' big data products are united under a brand called AnalytX, which powers various maintenance applications designed to optimise and improve aircraft usage. One app is Airplane Health Management (AHM), which uses predictive alerts to let operators ≫

Non-stop to Australia

One of the most notable routes the Boeing 787 flies is the first-ever regular non-stop service between Europe and Australia, a route from Perth to London Heathrow, operated by Qantas' fleet of 787-9s since December 2017. At around 17 hours long, depending on winds, the daily non-stop service covers 7,828 nautical miles, making it the longest yet served with a 787. Four pilots and 12 cabin crew operate the service.

A Qantas spokesperson told the author: "We're consistently seeing load factors in the 90s," (i.e., 90%-plus). The spokesperson said: "For Qantas, the capability and operating economics of the 787-9 means it is the perfect aircraft to carry out the non-stop flight between Australia and the UK. The route is very popular with our customers because of the incredible benefits the non-stop service offers and the enhanced cabin features, which really help minimise jetlag."

Qantas also operates its 787-9s to the United States on its Melbourne–Los Angeles, Melbourne–San Francisco and Brisbane–Los Angeles–New York JFK and Brisbane–Los Angeles routes. Qantas also flies the Dreamliner to Rome, Santiago and Paris.

evaluate two million parameters on the aircraft in real time, helping them schedule maintenance and minimise disruptions.

The AHM app is available across all Boeing commercial aircraft, not just the 787, but Boeing Global Services told the author one undisclosed customer has reduced turnaround times on its 787s by an average of 10% thanks to AHM. Qantas, United Airlines and Korean Air Lines are among 787 operators who have announced the use of AHM for their Dreamliners.

Another AnalytX-powered app on the 787 is Fuel Dashboard, which lets operators view and analyse fuel usage and adjust operations to improve efficiency. Boeing says the app, "routinely helps customers save between 4% and 7% on fuel costs, equating to millions of dollars in fuel savings and lower fuel emissions." There is a separate app for crew optimisation, designed to assist airlines in efficient rostering and crew planning based on real-time data to reduce operating costs by an average of three to 7%.

Trent 1000 engines on the production line at the Rolls-Royce plant in Derby, England. ROLLS-ROYCE

Boeing 787-9 G-VCRU (c/n 37972) is one of 17 delivered to Virgin Atlantic Airways seen on departure from London Heathrow Airport. AIRTEAMIMAGES/ SIMON WILLSON

Boeing Global Services said the company's resources, global presence and customer relationships gives it, "a unique ability to positively disrupt the market and generate a robust pipeline of products and services for 787 customers."

Further aftermarket support for the 787 provided by Boeing includes a landing gear exchange programme for managing landing gear overhauls. Following on from Boeing's history of similar programmes, 787 operators can exchange landing gear that　　　》

Delivered to Manchester International Airport on May 18, 2018, 787-9 G-TUIM (c/n 62742) is one of five in service with TUI Airways. TUI

Flying the 787

Boeing says a key strength of the 787 for operators is the aircraft's modern, advanced flight deck. Pilots clearly appreciate it, judging from comments provided to the author by several Dreamliner operators.

SIA, which now has seven years of Dreamliner operations under its belt after putting its initial 787-10s into service in March 2018, told the author: "The electronic checklist [ECL] is an extremely useful tool for pilots, guiding them as they carry out the necessary procedures. It replaces the conventional paper checklist and pilots can now access the checklist electronically to configure the aircraft systems for various stages of flight and conditions. In addition, the ECL minimises any mismanagement of lapses and omission of checklist items.

"The Boeing 787's flight deck features large landscape-format liquid crystal display screens and a vertical situational display. Pilots find the aircraft's handling to be agile and responsive. Operational excellence gained from one aircraft type can be seamlessly transferred to another with the high degree of cockpit commonality between the 787 and 777. Our cabin crew are trained in multiple aircraft fleets. Their experience in operating the 777 is certainly of benefit when they are cross-trained on the 787-10s."

TUI Airways said: "The flight deck is large and comfortable and very quiet compared to other aircraft. From a pilot's perspective, the aircraft is straightforward to operate and provides the pilot with several flight envelope protections adding to the safety of flight. The ECL provides the pilot with a simple and immediately accessible means of checklist completion. Some items in checklists are closed loop, which means that the system detects the position of a switch, lever or system and closes the loop automatically when an action has been taken. This means there are less items for the pilots to check.

"Dreamliners are equipped with dual HUDs [head-up displays] which provide the pilots with flight information in their line of sight, meaning that there is less of a requirement to look in. Full-time autothrottle capability and asymmetry compensation through the flight controls means that engine out handling is straightforward for the pilots."

Boeing 787 characteristics		
	787-8	**787-9**	**787-10**
Wingspan	197ft 3in (60.1m)	197ft 3in (60.1m)	197ft 3in (60.1m)
Length	186ft 1in (56.7m)	206ft 1in (62.8m)	224ft (68.2m)
Height	55ft 6in (16.9m)	55ft 10in (17.02m)	55ft 10in (17m)
Fuselage cross-section	18ft 10in (5.74m)	18ft 10in (5.74m)	18ft 10in (5.74m)
Max taxi weight	503,500lb (228,383kg)	561,500lb (254,692kg)	561,500lb (254,692kg)
Max take-off weight	502,500lb (227,930kg)	560,000lb (254,011kg)	560,000lb (254,011kg)
Max landing weight	380,000lb (172,365kg)	425,000lb (192,776kg)	445,000lb (201,849kg)
Max zero fuel weight	355,000lb (161,025kg)	400,000lb (181,436kg)	425,000lb (192,776kg)
Seats	242 dual-class (359 single-class)	290 dual-class (406 single-class)	330 dual-class (440 single-class)
Lower-deck cargo capacity	4,826ft³ (136.7m³) with space for 28 LD-3 containers	6,090ft³ (172.4m³) with space for 36 LD-3 containers	6,722ft³ (191.4m³) with space for 40 LD-3 containers
Usable fuel	223,378lb	223,773lb	223,773lb
Cruise speed	Mach 0.85	Mach 0.85	Mach 0.85
Range	7,355nm (13,620km)	7,635nm (14,140km)	6,430nm (11,910km)
Engines: Two General Electric GEnx-1B or Rolls-Royce Trent 1000	69,800lb (310kN) take-off thrust	74,100lb (329kN) take-off thrust	GEnx-1B generates 76,100lb (338kN) and the Trent 1000 TEN generates 78,000lb (347kN) take-off thrust

Source: Boeing Airplane Characteristics for Airport Planning

needs to be repaired or overhauled for another set of certified landing gear from a pool maintained by Boeing, eliminating the need for operators to contract, schedule and manage the overhaul process themselves.

Boeing also provides 787 type rating training at campuses that offer a mix of web learning, fixed based and full flight simulation. Full-motion 787 simulators are located at London Gatwick, Miami, Shanghai, and Singapore.

On Board Comfort

One of the much-heralded aspects of the 787 when it was launched was comfort for passengers thanks to the lower cabin altitude, the onboard filtration system and inlets drawing fresh air from the outside for air conditioning, LED mood lighting and larger windows.

China Southern Airlines operates Boeing 787-9 B-1188 (c/n 38797) which was the 787th Dreamliner built.
BOEING

According to TUI: "The cabin altitude is lower than on a conventional aircraft and the humidity is controlled to provide a fresher feel after the flight. Also, the windows on the aircraft are 30% larger than the conventional aircraft, making the cabin light and airy. There is no doubt that customers choose to fly on the Dreamliner because of these features."

Another big aspect of the flying experience for passengers is in-flight entertainment and connectivity (IFE&C). Widely available Wi-Fi, smartphones and other connected devices have raised travellers' expectations on connectivity and content and unsurprisingly airlines introducing the 787 ensure their Dreamliners are equipped with good IFE&C offerings.

For example, SIA 787-10s have an IFE&C system based around Panasonic's

eX3 system which the airline claims delivers a 'personalised interactive experience' enabling flyers to create playlists of movies and TV shows, receive media recommendations based on personal preferences and viewing history, and customise and search for entertainment options.

Virgin Atlantic 787-9s meanwhile are equipped with the Vera Touch 2, which offers 11in seatback screens in upper class (the airline's name for its first-class product) and premium economy and 9in screens for economy, with over 500 hours of entertainment (approximately 80 movies, 78 hours of TV and over 305 albums) with a shuffle option when listening to music and the facility to connect their own devices to the seatback system. All aircraft have exConnect, Ku band Wi-Fi from Panasonic. Customers with laptops, tablets, or mobile phones can connect their devices to the wireless onboard internet. ✈ 787

Australia's national carrier Qantas uses its 787-9s on its Perth to London Heathrow route, the first-ever regular non-stop service between Europe and Australia launched in December 2017.
QANTAS

Inside Boeing's huge Everett final assembly facility – this view shows three of four stations where 787s once took shape.
ALL PHOTOS BOEING UNLESS STATED

Building a Dream

Boeing created a supply chain of unprecedented length and complexity for the 787, with large components sourced from across the globe and delivered to the assembly lines at Everett and North Charleston, as **Paul Eden** explains.

Between them, Mitsubishi, Kawasaki and Fuji took a 15% work share in the 767-200/767-300 programme. Along with other Japanese suppliers, they then formed the Japan Aircraft Development Corporation and took a 20% stake in the 777, including responsibility for the entire fuselage (except the forward section), the wing centre section, wing to body fairings and assorted undercarriage and fuselage doors.

Other international suppliers, among them organisations from Australia, Brazil, Canada, France, South Korea and the UK, produce components that Boeing combines with its own items – plus those of other US manufacturers – to produce every 777.

Contrary to popular reporting, Boeing was no stranger to global supply chains when it came to manufacturing the Dreamliner. Where the 787 raised the bar, however, was in the scope of the international industrial and logistical co-operation required, because now the company expected aircraft sections to be complete with wiring, plumbing and other systems before they were delivered to its final assembly lines.

For the system to work, these sections had to be built with exceptional accuracy and arrive on time, ready for connection to other sub-sections that might literally have come from the other side of the world.

Another break from earlier programmes was entrusting detail

BELOW LEFT •
Components, including the horizontal tail section and vertical fin, are prepared ready for joining onto the Dreamliner's fuselage.

Positions 1a and 1b, where the forward and aft fuselage sections were once joined to the mid-body section on the Everett line.

Final assembly work is being carried on a jet for All Nippon Airways (ANA). After integration and systems checks are completed the 787 will then make its maiden flight.

design engineering to the partner companies, which would then produce sections of their own designs. This was a serious challenge for Boeing and its suppliers, and not all of them managed to achieve the standards required – in some instances Boeing representatives were obliged to intervene at a shop-floor level.

After considerable effort and not inconsiderable investment, the two 787 production lines, at Everett, Washington and North Charleston, South Carolina, were working more efficiently than ever. Taking into account that production struggled through much of 2014, it's quite remarkable that by the end of 2015 Boeing was able to report a 40% build cost reduction over the previous 240 aircraft deliveries.

Further production issues are avoided by a process of continuous risk assessment and analysis, as a Boeing spokeswoman explained to the author: "Through a combination of in-depth analysis, site visits and various metrics, including quality, parts availability and tooling readiness, we monitor and adjust to ensure production system health.

"Our supplier health assessment also involves financial cost trend analysis, quality, delivery and other performance metrics."

Production rate

In late February 2016, a 787 Supplier Management spokesperson confirmed that, between them, Everett and North Charleston were producing ten 787s a month, with a scheduled rate increase to 12 a month by mid-year.

Production continued to ramp up, but how could Boeing be sure the global »

Diagram showing the responsibilities of the major suppliers to the Dreamliner programme.

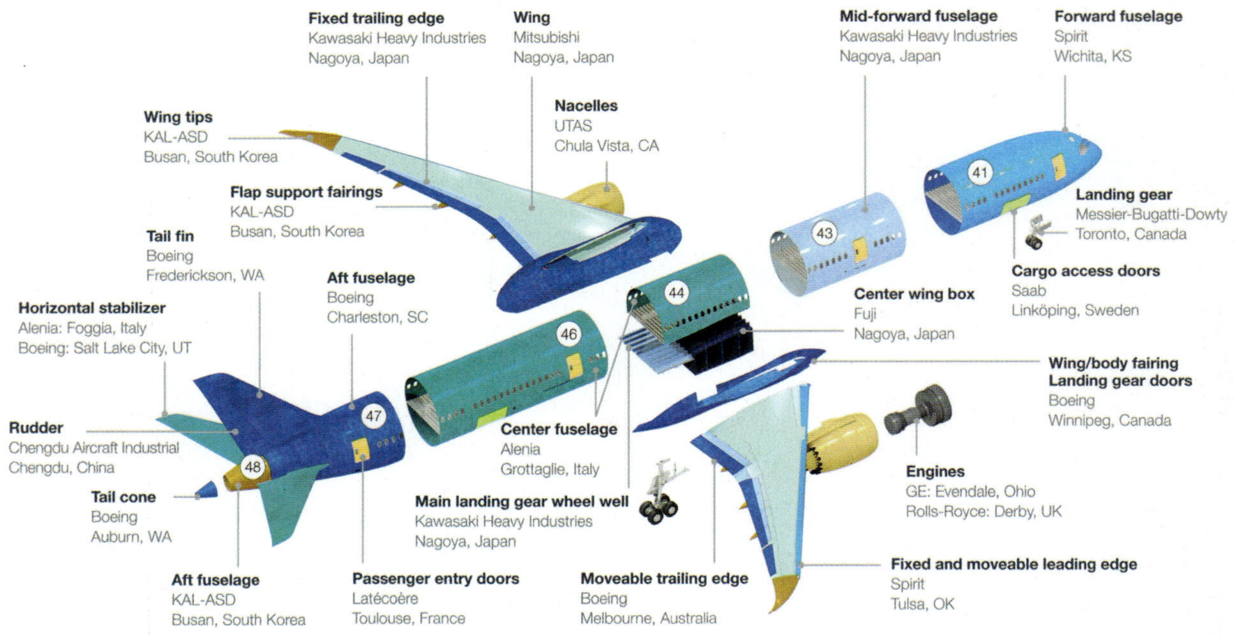

logistics chain would withstand building 787s more quickly without breaking?

"Rate readiness entails building detailed, comprehensive plans that define the actions, resources and timing required to successfully deliver the first aircraft at a new production rate," the spokeswoman said. "We work closely with our supplier partners to ensure they have the capacity, expertise and stability to meet our planned production rate increases now, and into the future. Our Supplier Management organisation rate readiness team is specifically focused on ensuring supplier readiness.

"To date we've generally found that suppliers are prepared for rate increases. In limited cases, we work with them to develop mitigation plans to address specific risks identified in the process."

Sum of all parts

The 787 supply chain initially delivered components only to Everett for final assembly, but a second assembly line was added in 2011. Located at North Charleston, it falls under Boeing South Carolina, which traces its origins back to 2004 when Vought Aircraft Industries and Global Aeronautica occupied the site. A joint venture between Vought and Alenia North America, the latter was established to support the 787 programme.

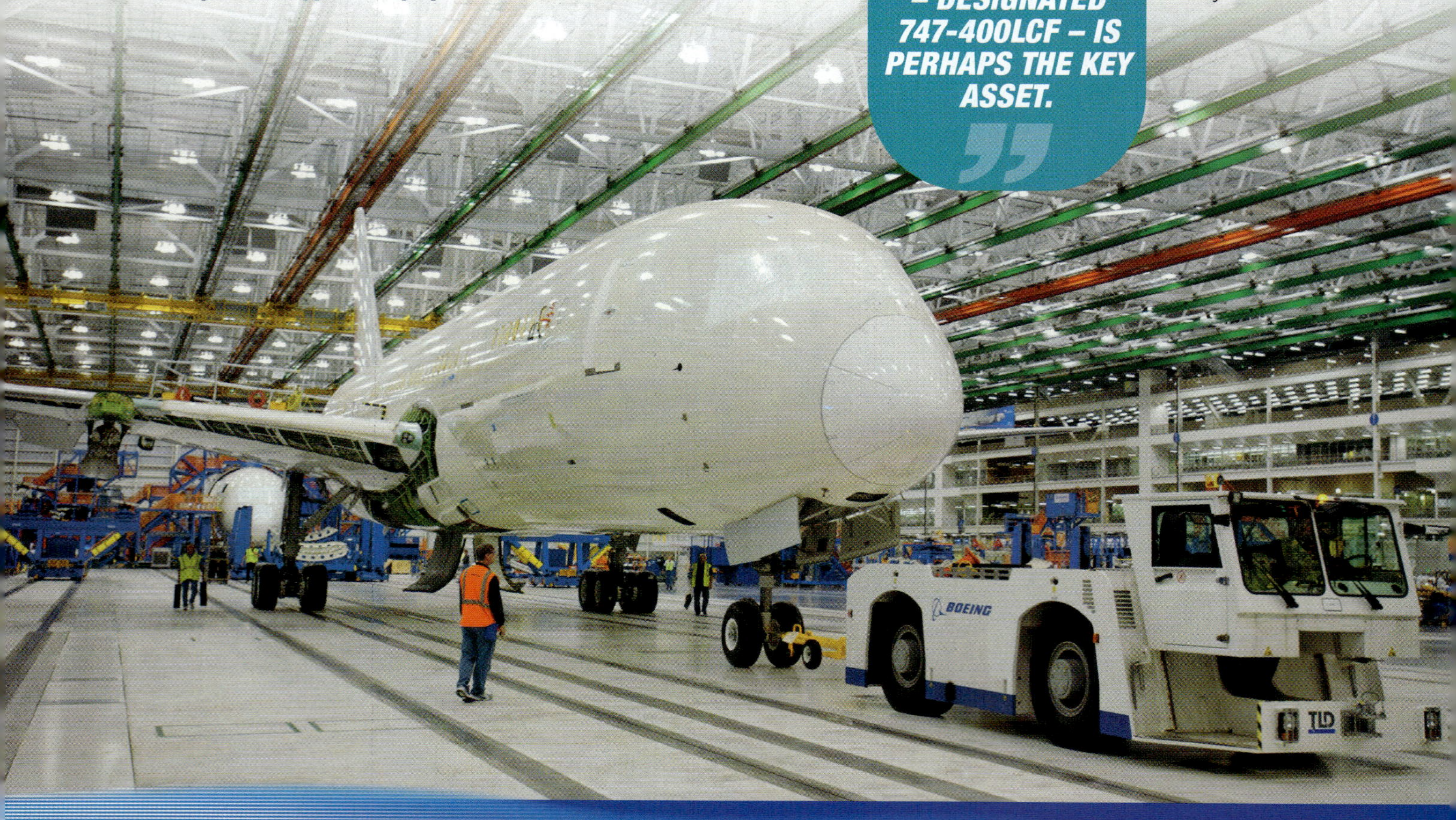

> **"ALTHOUGH ROAD, RAIL AND SEA TRANSPORT ALL HAVE IMPORTANT ROLES IN 787 PRODUCTION, THE DREAMLIFTER – DESIGNATED 747-400LCF – IS PERHAPS THE KEY ASSET."**

Boeing bought Vought's facility in July 2009, followed by its share in Global Aeronautica in December. The joint venture with Alenia was dissolved and the combination of the two assets created Boeing Charleston – now Boeing South Carolina.

Limited 787 production began in July 2011 and the

Now on its own undercarriage, this Dreamliner is towed to the next station in the final assembly process, where either its General Electric GEnx-1B or Rolls-Royce Trent 1000 engines are attached to the wings.

Major Supplier Responsibilities

Boeing sources components from 50 major suppliers across 135 sites.

Supplier	Components
Boeing Commercial Airplanes (Everett, Washington)	Development, integration, programme leadership
Boeing South Carolina (North Charleston)	Aft fuselage, mid-body integration, final assembly
Boeing Fabrication (Washington; Utah; Canada; Australia)	Fin assembly, moveable trailing edges, wing-to-body fairing, interiors
Boeing Interiors Responsibility Center (Washington; South Carolina)	Interior furnishing
Boeing Propulsion Systems Division (Washington)	Propulsion systems engineering and procurement services
Alenia Aermacchi (Italy)	Tailplane, centre fuselage
Spirit AeroSystems (Kansas and Oklahoma)	Fixed and movable leading edges, flight deck, part of forward fuselage, engine pylons
Fuji Heavy Industries (Japan)	Centre wing box, integration of centre wing box with main landing gear wheel well
Kawasaki Heavy Industries (Japan)	Main landing gear wheel well, main wing fixed trailing edge, part of forward fuselage
Mitsubishi Heavy Industries (Japan)	Wing box
United Technologies (Connecticut)	Auxiliary power unit, environmental control system, remote power distribution units, electrical power generating and start system, primary power distribution, nitrogen generation, ram-air turbine, emergency power system, electric motor hydraulic pump subsystem
Rockwell Collins (Iowa)	Displays, communications/surveillance systems, pilot control system
Honeywell (Arizona)	Navigation, maintenance/crew information systems, flight control, electronics, exterior lighting
GE Aviation (UK)	Common core system, landing gear actuation and control system, high-lift actuation system
United Technologies (North Carolina)	Fuel quantity indicating system, nacelles, proximity sensing system, electric brakes, exterior lighting, cargo handling system, flight deck lighting system, cabin attendant seating, fire protection system
Messier-Bugatti-Dowty (France/Canada)	Landing gear structure, electric brakes
Dassault Systèmes (France)	Global collaboration tools/software and (Michigan; Minnesota) software
Eaton Aerospace (UK)	Pumps and valves
Rolls-Royce (UK)	Engines
General Electric (Ohio)	Engines
Moog (New York)	Flight control actuators
Toray Industries (Washington)	Prepreg composites
Thales (France)	Electrical power conversion, integrated standby flight display, in-flight entertainment system
Labinal Power Systems (France/Mexico)	Wiring
Parker Hannifin (Ohio)	Hydraulic subsystem
Latécoère (France)	Passenger doors
Zodiac Water & Waste Aero Systems (California)	Water and waste system
Zodiac Aerosafety Systems (New Jersey)	Escape slides
Zodiac Cabin Interiors (Washington)	Sidewalls, window reveals, cargo linings, door linings and door surrounds
Panasonic (Japan)	Cabin services system, in-flight entertainment system
Bridgestone (Japan)	Tyres
Ultra Electronics (UK)	Wing ice protection system
GKN Aerospace (UK)	Composite mat for wing ice protection system
Esterline/Korry (Washington)	Flight deck control panels
Ipeco (UK)	Flight deck seats
Diehl Luftfahrt Elektronik (Germany)	Main cabin lighting
Jamco (Japan)	Lavatories, flight deck interiors, flight deck door and bulkhead assembly, galleys
Securaplane (Arizona)	Wireless emergency lighting system
Donaldson Company (Minnesota)	Air purification system
Astronautics Corp of America (Wisconsin)	Electronic flight bag
CTT Systems (Sweden)	Zonal drying system
PFW (Germany)	Metallic tubing and ducting
Saab Aerostructures (Sweden)	Large cargo doors, bulk cargo doors and access doors
Korean Airlines – Aerospace Division (Korea)	Raked wingtips
PPG Aerospace (Alabama)	Electrochromic windows
Triumph Group (Texas)	Longerons, stringers, shear ties and frame assemblies

*TOP • **Inside a 787's fuselage during the build phase.***

*ABOVE • **The second and third Boeing 787-9s for British Airways, G-ZBKB (c/n 38617) and G-ZBKC (c/n 38621), undergoing final assembly at Everett.***
BRITISH AIRWAYS

first complete aircraft emerged from final assembly the following April. North Charleston also builds aft fuselage sections for all 787s; they are moved across the facility to the final assembly line and were once flown by Dreamlifter to Everett.

Although road, rail and sea transport all have important roles in 787 production, the Dreamlifter – designated 747-400LCF – is perhaps the key asset. Four of them range across the Pacific from Nagoya, Japan, to North Charleston; fly between Italy and North Charleston; and cross the US, linking Wichita, Kansas, and Salt Lake City, Utah, with the final assembly facility.

Each major 787 subassembly is allocated a section number. So the centre fuselage wing box is Section 45, for example, while Section 41 is the forward fuselage, including the nose.

Both the main landing gear wheel well (Section 11) and Section 45 are produced at Nagoya, where they are integrated before loading onto a Dreamlifter bound for North Charleston. Section 43, the mid-forward fuselage, is also manufactured in Nagoya.

Boeing South Carolina assembles the 787's mid-body by uniting Section 43 to Section 44 (the mid-centre fuselage section forward of the wing), the » integrated Sections 11/45 and Section 46 (the mid-centre fuselage section aft of the wing).

Section 46 and the centre rear fuselage pieces (Sections 47 and 48) are manufactured on site, while Alenia Aermacchi produces Sections 44 and 46 at Grottaglie, Italy. The complete mid-body and Sections 47/48 move across the North Charleston site to the final assembly line or were once flown by Dreamlifter to Everett.

Other major airframe components delivered direct to the assembly line by Dreamlifter include Section 41 from Spirit AeroSystems at Wichita, Kansas; and the tailplanes, which are sourced from Alenia Aermacchi's Foggia, Italy or Boeing Fabrication's Salt Lake City, Utah, facilities.

Dream becomes reality

On the final assembly lines, the increasingly complete airframes move through four positions. At Positions 1a and 1b the major airframe parts are combined during the 'final body join', then the wings, undercarriage and empennage are added. The aircraft then rolls on to Position 2 on its own wheels where secondary structures – including floors, electrical wiring and hydraulic lines – are installed. The engines are hung on the wings at Position 3 and the aircraft is powered

The once 787 final assembly line at Everett, Washington.

up (electrically) for initial system tests. Further testing continues at Position 4 and the cabin interior is installed. From Position 4 the newly created airliner is rolled out to the paint shop.

Having made pioneering use of composites in the Dreamliner design, Boeing was obliged to create new technologies for its construction. Because large composite sections are preformed, far fewer holes for fasteners are drilled in the 787's fuselage during

final assembly than in a conventional 'aluminium' airliner – 10,000 in fact, compared with one million for a 747, according to Boeing.

Unlike metallic components, composite parts are formed (by a variety of processes) directly into the final shape required, whereas traditional manufacturing processes generally begin with a large block of metal that's machined into the final rough shape and then further worked on before incorporation

Boeing 747-400LCF Dreamlifter

Boeing commissioned Evergreen Aviation Technologies Corporation in August 2007 to convert four 747-400 airliners to 747-400LCF Dreamlifter configuration at its Taipei, Taiwan facility. A former Air China aircraft, two from China Airlines and one from Malaysia Airlines were chosen, the first completing its post-modification test flight on September 9, 2006. Two Dreamlifters entered service in 2007, the others following in 2008 and 2010. With a main deck cargo volume of 65,000cu ft (1,840m³), each aircraft can accommodate a pair of 787 wings or a full mid-body section. Loading and unloading is via the Dreamlifter's swing tail and uses a tail support and specialist loader, both developed for the purpose by Boeing.

One of the four Boeing 747s being converted into its Dreamlifter configuration. The work was carried out by Evergreen Aviation Technologies Corporation at its Taipei, Taiwan facility.

A specially developed cargo loader is used to remove 787 fuselage sections from the rear of a Boeing 747-400LCF Dreamlifter.

Boeing's Dreamlifter Fleet

Type	Reg	c/n	Del	Previous Operator
747-400LCF	N249BA	24309	Jul 08	China Airlines
	N718BA	27042	Feb 10	Malaysia Airlines
	N747BC	35879	Sep 06	Air China
	N780BA	24310	Mar 07	China Airlines

into the airframe – a massive and inescapably wasteful process the use of composite parts avoids.

However, even the seemingly simple task of drilling holes in huge composite fuselage and wing sections required new technology, for which Boeing commissioned Plano, Texas-based industrial automation and tooling specialists Advanced Integration Technology. The company built automated drilling machines that precisely prepare airframe sections for connection, using fasteners specially designed for the Dreamliner.

The result is an aircraft with all the structural integrity required of an airliner, but at a fraction of the weight of previous generation jets.

Anyone familiar with an airliner production line will be used to seeing incomplete aircraft in shades of bare metal or green primer, which is applied to protect aluminium sections on the line. For the Dreamliner, white is the prevalent shade, produced by a coating applied to protect the composites from UV radiation.

The final stage of production, before flight test and customer inspection, is painting. Between 500 and 600lb (227 and 272kg) of polyurethane paint is usually required to finish a 787, applied over a five-day period – unless the scheme is particularly complex, when finishing takes longer.

> **HAVING MADE PIONEERING USE OF COMPOSITES IN THE DREAMLINER DESIGN, BOEING WAS OBLIGED TO CREATE NEW TECHNOLOGIES FOR ITS CONSTRUCTION.**

An aerial view of Boeing's North Charleston facility. The third member of the Family, the -10, was and continues to be exclusively built here.

The completion of the first airframe off Boeing's second Dreamliner assembly line in North Charleston in 2012 was a major boost to the 787 programme.

Boeing 787 Dreamliner
An Overview

Following Boeing's consolidation of Dreamliner production at its North Charleston facility in March 2021, all 787 aircraft are now assembled, prepared for first flight, and delivered to the customer from the South Carolina base. Boeing has one consistent and thorough process for ensuring the quality of every Dreamliner before delivery.

Once a 787 rolls out of the factory, the delivery process begins. Though the amount of time it takes to deliver a 787 varies from customer to customer, the process always involves these steps:

- Painting and weighing
- Fuelling
- Preparing for and conducting first flight
- Preparing the aircraft for delivery
- Certifying, ticketing, and delivering the aircraft

Once a delivery date is set between the customer and Boeing, a detailed schedule is established that considers many variables, including the customer's needs and even cultural traditions.

Painting and Weighing

When a 787 aircraft rolls out from final assembly, it's already painted with a ready-to-go topcoat. This coating is applied to protect the aircraft's composite fuselage from ultraviolet light.

Once assembled, the aircraft is towed into the paint hangar, where a crew of a dozen or more painters apply between 500 and 600lb of polyurethane paint on a typical paint scheme. The actual painting process takes approximately five days, which includes one day for sanding the topcoat to prepare the aircraft for painting. More complicated liveries require additional time.

The Boeing facility in North Charleston has two paint hangars.

Once the aircraft is painted and decals and other placards are applied, it is weighed inside the paint hangar using a portable aircraft digital scale. The aircraft must meet a specific weight target required by the customer at delivery. Before the airline's crew can fly the jet home, more work must be done — the aircraft must be fuelled, assessed, and flown and the regulatory paperwork completed.

Boeing rolled-out the first Dreamliner assembled at the North Charleston facility on April 27, 2012. The jet, VT-ANI (c/n 36277) was built for Air India. BOEING

Mark Ayton selects highlights from background information about the Dreamliner provided by the manufacturer.

Fuelling

When a 787 aircraft is moved to the fuel dock, the team takes the aircraft through a series of tests to validate that the fuel system plumbing, pumps, valves, tanks, and flight-deck controls operate correctly. Other systems such as the fuel quantity indicating system and refuelling control panel, and hardware such as the jettison nozzles, are evaluated to ensure they work properly. The fuel is also assessed three different ways to ensure cleanliness of the system and the auxiliary power unit is started for the first time while these tests are under way.

Aviation maintenance technicians fill the aircraft's fuel tanks with Jet-A fuel, which is a type of aviation fuel designed for use in aircraft powered by gas-turbine engines. The aircraft is also defueled to check that the defuel pumps work properly and that the scavenge system in the centre fuel tank pushes fuel to the wings.

The quantity of fuel provided when the aircraft is delivered varies from customer to customer; however, on average, a 787 has 91,000lb of Jet-A fuel at the end of the fuel-testing process. Before the aircraft leaves the fuel dock, a standby compass calibrator is installed. The aircraft is then towed to a compass rose, where technicians swing the compass to calibrate it. The aircraft then travels to a pre-flight stall to prepare for its first flight.

Preparing an Aircraft for First Flight

All systems on the aircraft must be assessed before delivery. The process starts with servicing: running the engines, ensuring that there is the right amount of nitrogen in the tyres and shock struts and checking the hydraulic fluids.

Inside the cabin, technicians double-check the seats, flip every switch, and push every button on the flight deck, test the in-flight entertainment system and make sure all interior fixtures are installed properly. It is not a superficial or cosmetic check: engineers must certify that the cabin meets all Federal Aviation Administration (FAA) regulations.

The first flight for any Boeing commercial aircraft is called a B1 or a Boeing flight. Both Boeing and FAA pilots are authorised by the FAA to certify the aircraft for operations. Only four people are authorised to be on board the B1 flight: two pilots, one systems operator and one systems analyst. Each person has a series of defined tasks to complete during the flight, which typically lasts 2.5 to three hours.

Before the aircraft leaves the ground for the first time, pilots conduct a rejected take-off to test the brakes. During this manoeuvre, the aircraft is brought to near take-off speeds and stopped abruptly. Upon successful completion, the aircraft is ready to go.

Once airborne, the systems operator and analyst check that everything works the way it should. For example, every lavatory is checked — water turned on and off and toilets flushed — and every stow bin is opened and closed. The in-flight entertainment system is also checked.

As the crew heads back to the production site, the pilots disconnect the engine-driven generators to ⟩⟩

verify the ram-air turbine (RAT) works properly. The RAT, a small turbine connected to an electric generator, is one of the backup systems that ensure an aircraft can be safely landed even in the unlikely event of an engine failure.

The flight crew will document any issues — called flight squawks — during the B1 flight so they can be fixed before the customer's walk and final inspection. In some cases, additional Boeing flights are flown to verify that the aircraft is ready for delivery.

Preparing an Aircraft for Delivery

A customer's walk and final inspection occurs at the end of the process. Typically, a team from the airline arrives at Boeing to accept the aircraft several days before the contracted delivery date. The acceptance team may include pilots, flight operation personnel, a team of inspectors and typically a contracts representative.

Before the delivery, the airline's pilot, accompanied by a Boeing pilot, flies the 787 on a C1 — or customer flight — using the same profile flown on the B1 flight to test the systems and aircraft response once again. Sometimes specific airline requirements are also incorporated into the C1 flight plan.

Certifying, Ticketing and Delivering

Finally, the representatives from the customer and Boeing sign paperwork and settle the final payment for the new aircraft. On delivery day, airline executives and Boeing contracts specialists gather to do so in a conference room.

Every delivery is as individual as the customer. Some customers may elect to have an elaborate ceremony with high-level guests and media, while others may simply take the aircraft's ceremonial keys and fly the aircraft home.

Lifecycle Sustainability

Boeing has made steady progress throughout the jet age in improving the environmental performance of its aircraft, from fuel use

Boeing's North Charleston facility is part of the Charleston International Airport site and the co-located Charleston Air Force Base. BOEING

Boeing 787-8 c/n 36277 on take-off for its first flight from Charleston International Airport on May 23, 2012. BOEING

and emissions to community noise. With the 787 Dreamliner family, the company introduced new technologies to create even better lifecycle sustainability for commercial jetliners.

Boeing claims its commitment to improving sustainability is based on the company's deeply held belief that doing the right thing for the environment is also good business. This is especially true for an aircraft manufacturer because one of the many reasons that people choose to fly is to enjoy the variety of the world.

While this is an honourable commitment to make, the fact remains that Boeing wants to sell more aircraft. So, once the commercial airliner market recovers from the pandemic and geopolitical uncertainties, if Boeing sells 120 aircraft rather than 100, the 20% increase in sales helps to negate the efficiencies listed below.

Reduced Fuel Burn and Emissions Cut

Four key technologies on the 787 Dreamliner contribute to a 20 to 25% improvement in fuel use compared with the types of aircraft the 787 replaces: new engines, greater use of lightweight composite materials, more efficient systems applications, and modern aerodynamics.

Carbon dioxide (CO2) is produced as fuel is consumed. This means that reducing fuel use brings an equivalent reduction in CO2 emissions. According to Boeing, since the first 787 entered service in 2011, the 787 family has avoided more than 90bn pounds of carbon emissions.

Another key emission standard for commercial jetliners is nitrogen oxides (NOx). Specific regulations have already been set for future aircraft, using a complex formula that is based on the thrust ratings of aircraft engines. The 787 family is significantly more efficient — 20 to 25% more efficient — than the types of aircraft it replaces.

Quieter Take-offs and Landings

As communities located near to airports are all too aware, reducing the noise created by aircraft take-offs and landings is an important measure of environmental performance. As with its commitments to reduce fuel use and thus emission odours, Boeing has also worked to reduce the sound footprint of its aircraft — the distance across which disturbing noise is heard.

The 787 Dreamliner family incorporates new technologies to ensure that no sound of 85 decibels — about the level of loud traffic heard from the side of the road — leaves the airport boundaries. In fact, the noise footprint of the 787 is more than 60% smaller than those of the types of aircraft it replaces. Technologies include acoustically treated engine inlets and chevrons (the distinctive serrated edges at the back of the engines) and other special treatments for the engines and engine casings.

Point-to-Point

The mission capability of the 787 Dreamliner also provides an environmental advantage, allowing airlines to offer more direct flights connecting mid-sized cities. The 787 family has allowed for more than 320 new non-stop routes that previously were not financially feasible. While other larger, twin-aisle aircraft have the range to accomplish such missions, they are too large to operate economically on routes between mid-sized cities. The mid-sized 787, however, can operate quite efficiently between such cities, eliminating the need for additional take-offs and landings.

Connecting people more directly to their destination offers several environmental benefits. A more direct route uses less fuel and thus produces fewer emissions. Likewise, fewer take-offs and landings reduce the total noise footprint. And, for those passengers who need to be at hub airports, removing pass-through traffic keeps airports and airways clearer. Studies show that of all passengers at large hub airports, depending on the location between 30 and 50% are transit passengers, creating congestion and other environmental impacts in a city that is neither their point of origin nor destination.

The 787 is designed to transport passengers and cargo from their city of origin to their final destinations in the most environmentally efficient manner.

Less Wasteful Production

Because the 787 is made primarily of carbon-fibre composite material, which is trimmed like cloth, manufacturing processes produce less scrap material and waste. Most aircraft are made primarily of aluminium, which must be milled and machined from large sheets or blocks to create aircraft structure. In general, as much as 90% of the raw aluminium used to create aircraft parts is turned into

Boeing and its partners developed serrated chevrons as part of the engine's nacelle design which are meant to lower noise both inside and outside the cabin. BOEING

scrap during the manufacturing process. Although this scrap can be recycled, it is better to prevent this waste whenever possible. The 787 composite solution enables this efficiency.

In addition, Boeing's design team is working to reduce or eliminate materials that are less desirable for environmental performance and worker well-being.

According to Boeing, the overall manufacturing and maintenance process for the 787 produces less waste and uses fewer harmful chemicals and agents.

End-of-Life Recycling

Boeing collaborates with companies around the world to put in place processes to allow the 787 to be recycled when it is eventually retired. Though the first retirements are likely 30 years away, it is important that preparatory work is done today.

Boeing partnered with ELG Carbon Fibre in December 2018 to recycle excess aerospace-grade composite material, which will be used by other companies to make products such as electronic accessories and automotive equipment. The agreement – the first of its kind for the aerospace industry – covers excess carbon fibre from 11 Boeing aircraft manufacturing sites and will reduce solid waste by more than a million pounds a year.

Environmentally Responsible Facilities

Boeing South Carolina, home to 787 Dreamliner final assembly and delivery as well as the aft body and mid-body production facilities, became a 100% renewable energy site in 2011. Boeing South Carolina is also a zero waste-to-landfill site, meaning that no waste generated at the site is sent to landfill. Waste material is recycled, reused, repurposed, or sent to energy recovery facilities. 787

Boeing's paint facility at North Charleston, South Carolina. It opened in December 2016. BOEING

Powering
the Dreamliner

Boeing offers the 787 with a choice of two engines – from GE Aviation and Rolls-Royce. **Chris Kjelgaard** and **Mark Ayton** profile the powerplants.

After settling on its Super-Efficient Airliner concept in the early 2000s, Boeing made it immediately clear that its new mid-sized twin engine jet would be significantly more fuel efficient than the 767 it was replacing. This requirement was driven in part by the airline industry, which was shifting from the traditional hub-and-spoke model to point-to-point networks, and the growing emphasis on reduced operating costs.

Achieving this aim demanded major advances in the overall aircraft design with a substantial portion of this burden given to the new propulsion system.

Boeing approached two manufacturers – GE Aviation (GE) and Rolls-Royce (RR) – with an ambitious brief to improve fuel burn and introduce significant architectural innovations such as the use of advanced materials and replacing the heritage bleed air system. Additionally, the powerplant had to meet more stringent noise and emissions requirements, to maximise the capital value of the airframe, and should be designed to be fully interchangeable with the other engine type.

The result – the GE Aviation GEnx-1B and Rolls-Royce Trent 1000 – represents a full two-generation jump in technology over the 767 and is the biggest contributor to the 787's overall fuel-efficiency improvements.

GEnx-1B

Launched in 2004, the GEnx high-bypass, large-turbofan engine family powers two different aircraft types, both produced by Boeing. The GEnx-1B is one of two engines for the 787, while the -2B is the sole-choice powerplant for the 747-8 Intercontinental and Freighter aircraft.

The latter engine has a slightly smaller fan diameter, a lower bypass

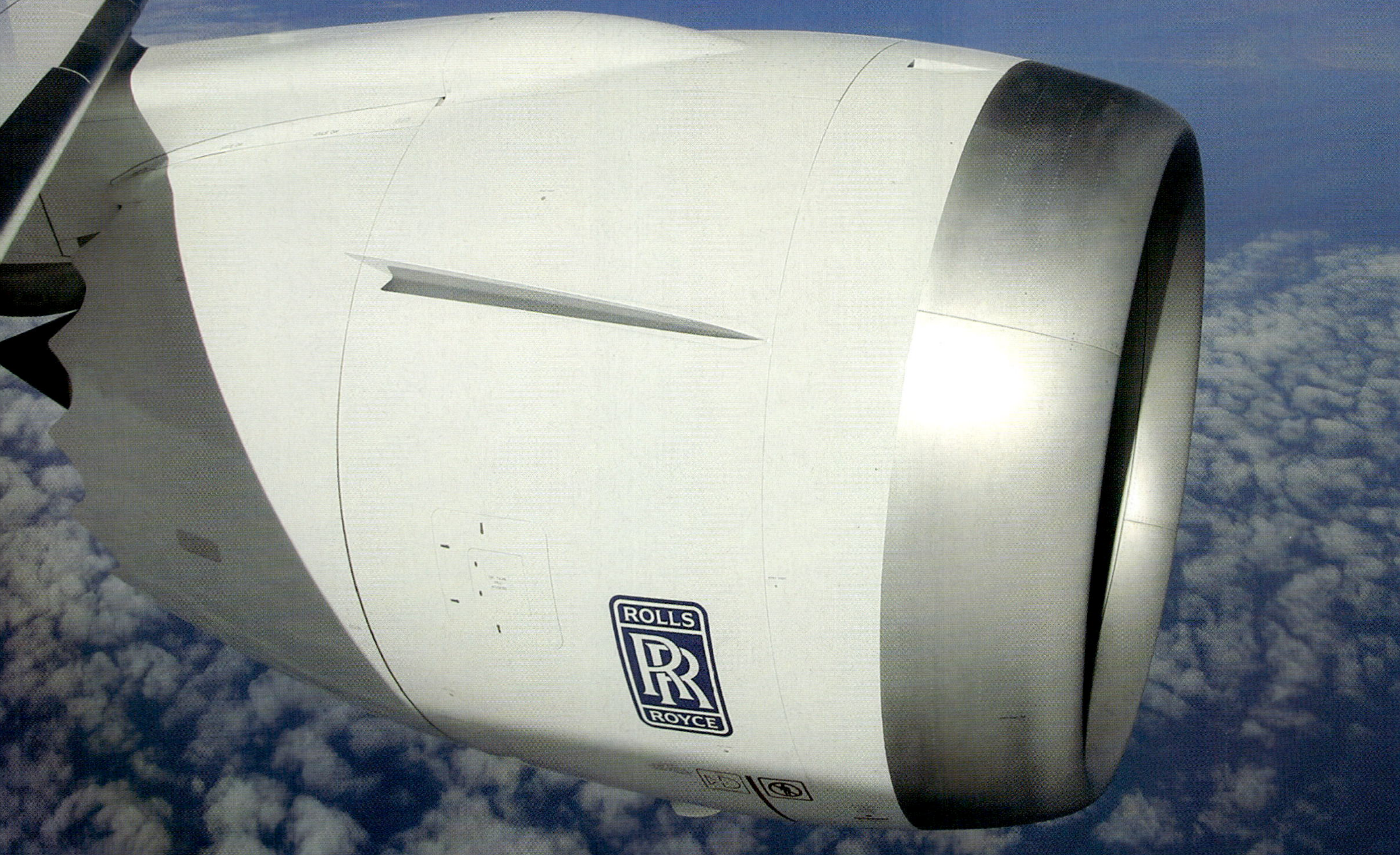

Boeing 787 Dreamliner launch customer All Nippon Airways selected the Rolls-Royce Trent 1000 to power its 80+ fleet of 787-8 and 787-9 aircraft. AIRTEAMIMAGES.COM/KSK

ratio and one fewer low-pressure (LP) compressor and LP turbine stages than the GEnx-1B. However, the most notable difference between the two variants is that the -1B is 'bleedless' – unlike most current-generation types, the all-electric Dreamliner does not use compressed air bled from the engines to power aircraft systems.

The GEnx-1B family was certificated at 78,000lb maximum take-off thrust which is more than sufficient to power even the largest member of the Dreamliner family, the 787-10. It also means that all variants of the -1B powerplant (see table) are identical in terms of materials and components. The different maximum-thrust limits are instead achieved via software in the aircraft's full authority digital engine control (FADEC) computers.

Like almost every other large-turbofan (except for the RR RB211 and Trent families), the GEnx has a two-shaft design. The low pressure (LP) shaft is driven by the LP turbine stages near the back of the powerplant and turns the fan at the front. This produces large amounts of cold and relatively slow-moving bypass air, which accounts for almost all the engine's thrust.

The 111.1in diameter fan is a technological highlight. Each fan blade is made of layers of carbon-fibre composite threads woven into a complex swept design that is extremely strong and aerodynamically efficient. GE first developed composite fan

blades for the previous generation GE90 family, which entered service on the 777 in 1995. However, those used on GEnx-1B are so efficient the manufacturer was able to reduce the total number of fan blades from 22 to 18.

Each blade features a stainless-steel leading edge to increase resistance to foreign object damage (FOD). The engine is also equipped with a system that diverts all compressor-bound FOD into the bypass airflow via the variable bleed valve doors (VBVs, located between the low- and high-pressure compressor modules). The inward-opening VBVs also unload the high-pressure (HP) compressor when the engine is

commanded to increase power quickly, enabling the GEnx to spool up and preventing any compressor stall.

Additionally, the GEnx engine introduced the intermetallic chemical compound material called Titanium Aluminide (TiAL) in stage 6 through 8 LP turbine blades. This reduced the engine's weight by 400lb compared with the materials used on the similar thrust class GE CF6-80C2. TiAL is both lightweight with low ductility, and resistant to oxidation and heat.

The engine's second shaft – the HP shaft – connects the ten HP compressor and two HP turbine stages. Between these two modules lies GE's advanced »

Before an engine is attached to the wing it undergoes a series of tests. Here the manufacturer conducts icing trials on a GEnx engine at its Winnipeg facility.
GENERAL ELECTRIC AVIATION

The Rolls-Royce Trent 1000 is the fifth generation of the engine optimised specifically for the Dreamliner.
ROLLS-ROYCE

'twin-annular pre-swirl' (TAPS) combustor, which mixes fuel with hot, highly compressed air entering from the HP compressor before injecting the resultant vapour through nozzles spaced evenly around the engine's two combustor rings.

This pre-mix method ensures the mixture burns evenly throughout the combustor and at a relatively low temperature, reducing the amount of nitrogen oxide produced to levels far below those mandated by ICAO and helps the engine's fuel efficiency compared to its similar thrust class predecessor engines, the CF6-80E1 and CF6-80C2.

When the GEnx-1B was evaluated on the 787-8, community noise certification levels were 40% lower than the Boeing 767's GE CF6-80C2 engine.

GE employed advanced 3D designs in the high-pressure portion of the engine, including one-piece bladed discs (dubbed 'blisks') on the first, second, and fifth compressor stages. These replace conventional rotors – each with hundreds of blades and heavy titanium bases – and are much lighter, stronger, and more reliable.

The GEnx is also GE's first engine to incorporate a fan case made from carbon fibre composites rather than the traditional aluminium. Not only is this stronger and more durable but, according to GE, it is also 350lb lighter.

Certification

GEnx-1B engines completed the first flight on a Boeing 787 on June 16, 2010, at Paine Field in Everett, Washington following five years of testing.

The FAA issued type certification for the GEnx-1B's Performance Improvement Package I (PIP I) on August 12, 2011. PIP 1 includes a redesign of the low-pressure turbine air foils to provide a substantial improvement to specific fuel consumption. At the time, GE was evaluating the PIP II which includes upgrades to the high-pressure compressor to bring additional fuel consumption improvements.

On December 1, 2011, the FAA granted 330-minute extended-range, twin-engine operations (ETOPS) approval to the GEnx-1B engine following a 3,000-cycle ground endurance test in April 2011. The agency subsequently granted 330-minute extended-range, twin-engine operations (ETOPS) approval of the GEnx-1B Performance Improvement Program (PIP) engine on March 8, 2012. At the time of the PIP certification, Boeing had completed all flight tests of the GEnx-powered Boeing 787 aircraft as required for FAA type certification: the baseline GEnx-1B and PIP engine had already received FAA engine certification.

In July 2012, GE Aviation announced it was continuing to assess the GEnx engine to accumulate an additional 25,000 cycles by 2016, equivalent to 20 years of service, as part of its maturation programme.

By November 29, 2012, 40 GEnx-1B engines in operation had recorded 33,000 hours and 6,700 cycles, and had, according to GE performed better than expected.

At the time, the second element of the two-stage PIP intended to ensure the GEnx-1B meets fuel-burn requirements and provides higher levels of thrust needed to support growth in aircraft weight, dubbed PIP II were near completion. Testing was completed in early 2013, followed by FAA airworthiness approval. The PIP II package added various fan, booster, compressor, and combustor changes to the low-pressure turbine improvements covered by PIP I.

After 37 flights, GE completed GEnx-1B PIP-related work on its Boeing 747 flying testbed and delivered flight-test engines to Boeing. In a six-year development programme, GE assessed more than 50 GEnx engines, logged 38,000 ground and flight cycles and accumulated 43,000 hours of engine-running experience.

Dust Ingestion Testing

In 2021, GE conducted endurance testing on a heavily instrumented production standard GEnx-1B engine in a specialised dust ingestion rig at its Peebles, Ohio test facility. The instrumented engine was removed in September after completing 3,005

A technical cutaway drawing showing the main components that make up a Trent 1000 engine. ROLLS-ROYCE

The Trent 1000 is being continually improved by Rolls-Royce, with various upgrade packages enhancing both fuel-burn and thrust. ROLLS-ROYCE

simulated flight cycles in a simulated severe environment with mimicked dust so fine that it is invisible.

Each flight cycle simulated operating speeds and temperatures experienced during take-off, climb, cruise, descent, and landing/thrust reverse phases of flight. The engine was allowed to cool down between operations to mimic the time between flights.

An improved combustor deflector and a redesigned stage 1 HPT blade were the focus of the test, because they are more sensitive to dust ingestion in harsh environments, but GE engineers also evaluated durability improvements to

> **THE TRENT IS THE ONLY MODERN COMMERCIAL TURBOFAN TO FEATURE A THREE-SHAFT DESIGN...**

other components, including fuel nozzles and fuel system components.

GE engineers spent months determining the dust constituents and flow rates by analysing ground and air samples collected in different regions of the world. Flow rates were varied as the engine transitioned through the different simulated phases of flight. In some instances, depending on flow rate, humidity level and lighting, the dust flow was visible.

By using current production parts mixed with the improved components during the test, GE engineers were able to monitor progression of oxidation and wear. The engineers were also able to compare the test data with data found in the field as a means of confirming the test conditions.

Dust injection rates were accurately measured and controlled on the dust rig itself through a patented injection system. GE engineers were able to validate dust accumulation by comparing BSI results of the endurance engine to actual customer engines operating different regions of the world.

GE Aviation told the author its engineers used lean principles to improve the findings of the test campaign. GE engineers worked for many months to perfect the dust ingestion equipment to ensure the test closely simulated actual flight conditions. Several trials were conducted, collecting data, analysing results, and making improvements to be certain the test conditions matched the conditions of different regions of the world.

The GEnx is known for its reliability, which lead to higher availability and utilisation before the COVID-19 pandemic, when operators were eager to fly every available aircraft at every opportunity they could.

Based on statistics generated by flight tracking website FlightRadar24, in 2019 GEnx-powered Dreamliners flew 6% more days than other competition-powered 787s. According to GE Aviation, that means that on average, a GEnx-powered 787 flies seven more days per year than competition-powered aircraft. Consequently, GEnx-powered Dreamliners provide operators with more revenue potential thanks to the aircraft's utilisation rates.

By March 1, there were over 1,500 GEnx-1B series engines in service, with 49 operators representing 68% of the Dreamliner fleet. These had accumulated a combined 23.8 million flying hours across 3.9 million cycles for the fleet. The highest cycle engine has 6,530 cycles and the highest time engine has 35,200 flight hours, both since new.

Since its 2011 introduction, the GEnx engine (including the GEnx-1B and GEnx-2B models) accumulated orders for nearly 2,800 units, making it GE's fastest selling wide body commercial aircraft engine.

Trent 1000

The Trent 1000 is the fifth generation of the Rolls-Royce (RR) Trent engine family and, according to the Derby-based firm, was optimised specifically for the Dreamliner.

The GEnx-1B is the leading engine choice for airline's ordering the Boeing 787, with General Electric Aviation claiming a 99.96% dispatch reliability and a 25% lower engine removal rate than its competitor.
GE AVIATION

Close-up detail of the General Electric GEnx-1B engine.
GE AVIATION

In keeping with its heritage, the powerplant, which produces between 69,000lb and 78,000lb of thrust at take-off power, retains the same three-shaft design as its stablemates. The LP shaft, which is driven by six LP turbine stages, turns the 20-blade fan – with a diameter of 112in, the fan is as wide as the fuselage of Concorde!

The Trent is the only modern commercial turbofan to feature a three-shaft design that, RR claims, makes the engine shorter, stiffer, lighter, and more resistant to FOD than the equivalent two-shaft design.

The Trent 1000 weighs approximately 6 tonnes, contains over 18,000 individual components and, at take-off power, pushes out 2,840lb of air per second. Around 85% of the thrust generated by the engine is cold bypass air.

Like the GEnx-1B, the Rolls-Royce powerplant also provides an electrical power offtake but, unlike the GE engine, the Trent 1000 does so from the intermediate rather than the HP shaft. RR says this translates to a lower engine idling speed and, consequently, lower fuel burn.

The British engine has the distinction of powering the maiden flights of the 787-8, 787-9 and 787-10, was the first to achieve certification and the first to enter commercial service on all three variants. The latest and current production version of the engine is the Trent 1000-TEN (Thrust, Efficiency and New Technologies) which powers all three variants of the 787 Dreamliner.

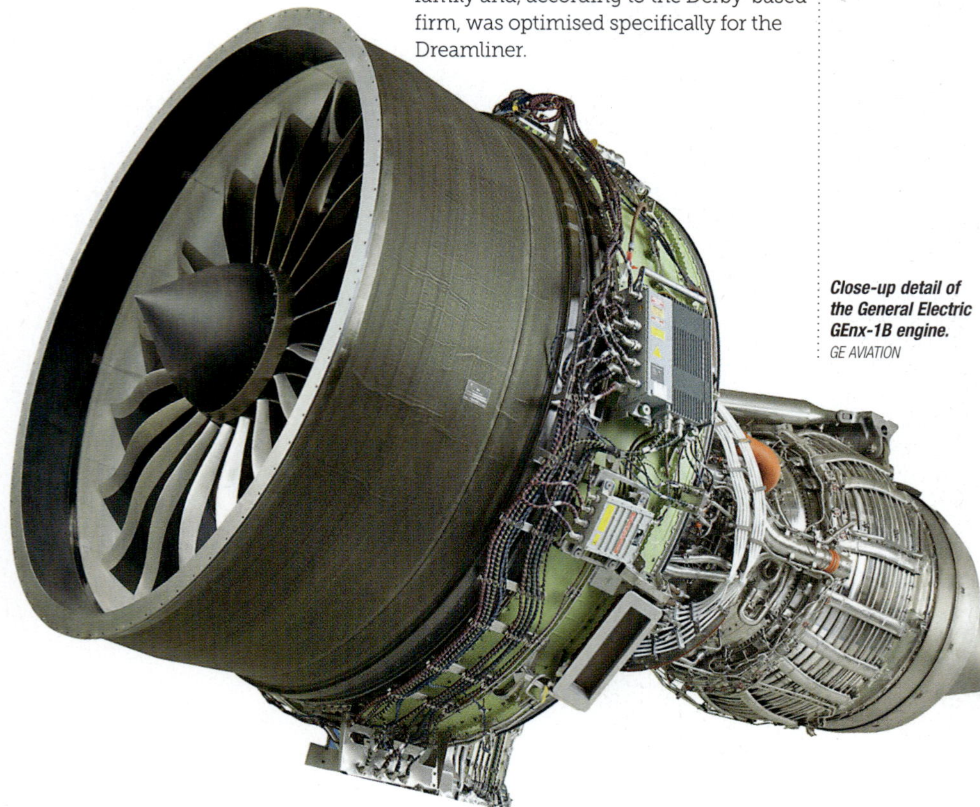

Trent 1000 TEN

On June 3, 2014, RR announced the first run of a Trent 1000-TEN engine. At the time, demonstrator programmes had already validated improvements to the high-pressure turbine, compressors and internal air systems.

By March 2016, the Trent 1000 TEN engine had flown for the first time on RR's Boeing 747 flying test bed aircraft, N787RR (c/n 21966) *Spirit of Excellence*, at Tucson, Arizona. The engine installed on the 747 was the eighth Trent 1000 TEN engine produced. The flight test programme comprised 100 hours of flying.

RR installs test engines on the inboard pylon of the 747 test-bed, which is equipped with instrumentation to allow engine performance measurements to be recorded in flight. Operating a test engine on the 747 allows testing that's not possible on the ground and ensures the engine is ready for flight test operations on 787 Dreamliner aircraft.

In addition to completing certification type testing, Trent 1000 TEN test engines underwent more than 150 hours of hot and fast running designed to simulate conditions well beyond those encountered in regular service.

The Trent 1000 TEN engine received official certification from the European Aviation Safety Agency (EASA) on July 11, 2016, at Farnborough Airshow. Confirmation that the Trent 1000 had fulfilled EASA's airworthiness requirements.

Boeing Field in Seattle was the location for the first flight of a Dreamliner fitted with the ninth Trent 1000 TEN engine on December 8, 2016. The successful flight on the Boeing 787-8 development aircraft kicked-off the latest phase in the engine's development programme. This flight test programme was designed to verify engine performance and to confirm software integration with the aircraft.

This notable event was followed on March 31, 2017, with the first test flight of the 787-10 powered by Trent 1000 TEN engines. This completed a hat trick of accomplishments for the Trent 1000 engine which powered the first flight of all three versions of the 787.

Prior to an announcement on August 18, 2017, that the EASA granted the Trent 1000 TEN full flight certification, a 787-8 test aircraft powered by TENs completed an 18-hour test flight around the United States.

The TEN produces 78,000lb of thrust at maximum power but, in de-rated form, is also suitable for use on the smaller 787-8 and 787-9.

The Trent 1000 has been subject to continuous improvements since its entry into service, including two upgrade packages (B and C) that have delivered marked enhancements to fuel burn and thrust. The TEN delivers further upgrades. The newest variant incorporates much of the technology developed for the Airbus A350's Trent XWB including a new 'rising line' compressor design and the addition of blisks in the HP compressor. RR says the TEN has a 70-75% part change over the package C variant which includes a near-new core and new associated systems.

In-Service Issues

RR's 2017 full year results gave an account of in-service engine issues on the Trent 1000 caused principally by lower-than-expected durability of a small number of parts. RR reported that the issues required urgent short-term support including both on-wing and shop visit intervention which caused increased disruption for some customers. RR said it had made progress in its understanding of both the technical and operational issues and had come up with longer-term solutions, primarily through re-designing affected parts. This date was pushed back still further, and in 2025, some airlines were still reporting issues with the engine.

On April 13, 2018, RR provided an update on the Trent 1000 in-service issues. As part of its ongoing inspection and testing of the affected engines, the company had decided to conduct additional engine inspections to those previously planned. RR said: "The increased inspection frequency is driven by our further understanding of the durability of the Trent 1000 package C compressor. These inspections will be supported by service management and flight operations guidance to airlines to be issued by the airworthiness authorities. This will unfortunately lead to additional disruption for our customers. There are 380 package C engines currently in-service with airlines. This new regime does not impact Trent 1000 package B engines or Trent 1000 TEN engines."

Since the Airworthiness Directive mandating additional intermediate compressor inspections was introduced in April 2018, RR trebled the number of affected engines worked on at any point. This was achieved by developing and introducing lean work scope methods, which allowed RR engineers to reduce the time an engine spends in maintenance. Further maintenance, repair and overhaul lines were opened to provide for the work to take place.

RR also accelerated the development of the permanent fix to the issue with the intermediate pressure compressor (IPC) blade seen on package C engines, and a »

In October 2015, General Electric Aviation completed the 1,000th GEnx engine, just five years after the first production version was built at the manufacturer's Durham facility in North Carolina.
GE AVIATION

GEnx Facts

- At the time of its entry into service, the GEnx-1B had the highest overall pressure ratio in commercial service at 55.4:1. The GE9X, GE's newest wide body commercial engine set to power the Boeing 777X aircraft, boasts an overall pressure ratio of 60:1.
- GE's lean burn TAPS combustor technology enables the GEnx to have ten times the margin for NOx Vs the standards set at the eighth meeting of the committee on aviation environmental protection, dubbed CAEP/8 vs its thrust class predecessor engines, the CF6-80E1 and CF6-80C2.
- In terms of reliability, according to GE Aviation the GEnx-1B has a removal rate that is one third that of its competitor, the Rolls-Royce Trent 1000. Additionally, the in-flight significant event rate (diversions and turn backs while airborne) is half that of competitor-powered 787s. Lastly, the GEnx has maintained a reliability advantage over the competing engine since the 787 entered service.
- In terms of lowest fuel burn, according to GE Aviation a GEnx-1B PIP2-powered 787-9 is 1.4% more efficient than a Rolls Royce Trent 1000 TEN-powered aircraft for a 3,000nm mission. The GEnx engine holds a fuel burn advantage over the Trent TEN for all 787 missions greater than 750nm. Such fuel efficiency means that a 787 powered by GEnx engines can carry the same load of passengers and cargo and fly 115 nautical miles further than a Trent-powered aircraft.
- In respect of time-on-wing and durability of the GEnx, GE is still investing in improving the engine's durability even though the GEnx has a three-time TOW advantage compared with the Trent 1000. GE has active programmes aimed at improving the durability of hot section and fuel system components, and other parts that drive maintenance actions for operators. Two examples that seek to lower maintenance costs are the use of lightweight durable materials and advanced design processes. GE continues to increase the use of advanced lightweight materials such as carbon fibre composites and ceramic matrix composites. Both materials are lighter but provide greater strength and durability.
- Australian national carrier Qantas has undertaken some record-setting flights with its GEnx-powered Boeing 787s. On March 24, 2018, Boeing 787-9 VH-ZND flew the 17-hour and 20-minute flight between Perth Airport, Australia, and London-Heathrow where it landed the following day.
- In October 2020, a Qantas 787-9 with 49 passengers and crew on board flew a 10,200-mile, 19-hour and 16-minute research flight from New York-JFK to Sydney as part of Project Sunrise.
- On October 7, 2021, a Qantas 787-9 with 107 passengers on board flew a 9,200 mile, 17-hour and 25-minute repatriation flight from Buenos Aires, Argentina to Darwin. This record setting flight was the longest commercial flight in the 100-year history of Qantas.

redesigned blade was installed in a test engine and assessed.

New on-wing inspection techniques to support airlines in meeting the requirements of the Airworthiness Directives were quickly developed, and development of the permanent fix for the issue was accelerated.

To meet and exceed a single digit aircraft on ground (AOG) target by mid-2020, RR also increased the availability of spare engines to ensure greater flexibility and security against operational disruption.

Its policy to constantly monitor the health of in-service engines, progressively identified the durability issues affecting some parts on the Trent 1000 package B and package C engines which had worn out faster than forecast. Specifically, fatigue cracking on the intermediate pressure turbine (IPT) blades; deterioration in the condition of high-pressure turbine (HPT) and IPC rotor blades. The three issues happened concurrently.

IPT Blades

Some IPT blades were found to be affected by a form of chemical corrosion. Elevated temperatures found in the hot section of an engine react with pollutants in the air causing sulphidation. To improve engine durability, RR introduced a new IPT blade design manufactured from a more corrision resistant metal and featuring an improved protective coating.

Explaining the issue, Scott Holland, VP regional marketing at Rolls-Royce said: "The issue with the IPT blade was first discovered following an in-flight shutdown in 2015. For all issues that cause an operational impact, we invoke a robust system to investigate the root cause and subsequently put containment action in place while we work on a permanent solution.

"The engine was removed and sent to the overhaul shop, where it was stripped and investigated. Specifically, the failed IPT blade was removed and sent to RR's Derby laboratory for analysis.

This identified sulphidation as the root cause and discovered crack propagation originating from the corroded area near the root of the blade. With this understanding we implemented restrictive life management of the IPT blades in service based on predictive modelling and launched the development of a permanent solution."

Based on their experience with other models of the Trent engine which have IPT blades made with a different base metal, RR engineers were able to devise a solution. This included extending the protective coating further down the root of the blade to fully encapsulate the affected area.

However, in November 2024, Rolls-Royce said it was targeting FAA certification of a Trent 1000 high-pressure turbine blade (HPT) improvement "in the coming months", though by April 2025, this had not been confirmed.

HPT Blades

To improve durability of the HPT blades for package B and package C, RR had introduced a new HPT blade design in October 2018.

HPT blades are subject to routine on-wing borescoping to monitor their condition in service and this showed thermal distress and cracking at lower lives than expected. The cause of the cracking was higher temperatures than expected in certain areas on the blade surface. The HPT blade design features a thermal barrier coating and a technology called film cooling – which sees cooler air blown through tiny holes in the blade, each with its own size, direction and shape. Positioning of these cooling holes is critical to avoid hot spots. According to Scott Holland it takes just one area of the blade to be subjected to a higher temperature than expected, to cause deterioration of the coating and create cracking in that area He said: "Blades

GE conducted endurance testing on a heavily instrumented production standard GEnx-1B engine in a specialised dust ingestion rig at its Peebles, Ohio test facility. GE AVIATION

The Trent 1000 final assembly line at the manufacturer's Derby facility showing engines in various stages of the build process. *ROLLS-ROYCE*

removed from service were subject to lab analysis to understand the hot spot areas and compared against our design models to identify any discrepancies and inform a re-design."

The solution required new positioning of the holes so that all areas of the blade are washed with sufficient cooler air to maintain it at the right temperature during operation such that cracks do not initiate.

Scott Holland explained: "Certain areas of the blade are hotter than others, so positioning of the holes and how many, in the right place and pumping the right amount of cooler air at certain places around the blade is critical."

Separately following entry into service of the TEN, the condition of some HPT blades installed on a sub-set of the fleet were found to be deteriorating faster than expected and this necessitated an accelerated inspection regime. The investigation and findings were incorporated into the work already underway on an improved HPT blade for the Trent 1000 TEN. This new blade was due to be available later in 2022.

IPC Rotor Blade

Improvements were also required for the first and second stages of the IPC rotor blade. RR determined the IPC rotor blades could vibrate under certain conditions, which causes cracking. Initially the company introduced modified IPC blades for package C engines, which represents about half the Trent 1000 family's installed base.

RR also introduced a redesigned IPC blade for package B and Trent 1000 TEN engines. The blade for the TEN was certificated and put into new production in 2019 and the programme to install the new blades to engines that were already in-service was on-going. As of February 2022, this programme was around 60% complete.

The issue with the IPC blade was trickier to determine because the root cause was frequency coincidence between engine components.

Following a lot of service data analysis, testing and modelling, RR engineers determined that under certain operating situations and fan rotational speeds, the wake off the back of the fan entering the IPC created a forcing frequency that coincided with the natural frequency of the stage 1 and stage 2 IPC blades. The associated vibration induced stresses at the root of the blade, led to crack initiation. With this understanding the engineers were able to redesign the IPC blades so that their natural frequency falls outside of any operating frequency within the engine.

With large engines like the Trent 1000, for efficiency, the fan blades operate quite slowly, and the blades in the IPC are under little stress in a cool operating environment at the front of the engine. The unique characteristics of the Trent 1000, particularly the number of fan blades, the proximity of the fan blades to the front of the compressor, its operating speed at certain points of flight, in certain operations caused the frequency coincidence.

Implementing Fixes

The three in services issues affected the fleet concurrently, with the restricted lives driving engines off wing earlier than planned. This put pressure on the number of spare engines available resulting in AOG waiting for serviceable engines to be returned following repair or overhaul.

Once the fixes were certificated, and new, redesigned components were available, RR had to ensure the airlines sent their affected engines to an overhaul shop for installation in accordance with the fleet programme.

Before the COVID-19 pandemic, RR sought to reach a single-digit AOG count by mid-2020. However, the travel bans put in place because of the pandemic meant many airlines were unable to operate which allowed RR to push the engines through the overhaul facilities and return serviceable engines back to the customers. Consequently, RR achieved a zero AOG count by mid-2020 ahead of its original target allowing the company to re-establish and maintain a healthy level of spare engines with which to support operations worldwide. On June 12, 2025, Rolls-Royce announced the first of two Durability Enhancement Packages aiming to double the duration in service of the Trent 1000 before requiring maintenance. The programme began on new engines in January 2025, and the company said that the entire Trent 1000 fleet would be upgraded within two years.

A GEnx engine suspended on an assembly line track. *GE AVIATION*

Dreamliner Aircraft
INNOVATIONS

One of the biggest innovations in the 787 is the aircraft's cabin. The starting point for the interior's design came back in the early 2000s, before the Dreamliner programme was even launched. At that time, Boeing was working on the Sonic Cruiser and the company wanted to understand in greater detail what mattered to passengers to help it create the cabin for its new concept design.

As it turned out, the Sonic Cruiser was cancelled and the Super Efficient Airliner concept for a new mid-size aircraft was launched instead – but the work that had been carried out on understanding travellers' needs had a direct influence on the cabin of what eventually became the 787.

Blake Emery, then Director, Differentiation Strategy for Boeing Commercial Airplanes, recalled that initial consultations with fliers revealed "the deep psychological needs people have when they're inside an aircraft".

Research into those needs was conducted by Boeing with the Denmark Technical Institute near Copenhagen and the Oklahoma State University Centre for Health Sciences in Tulsa. These studies investigated how light, space, cabin air quality and pressurisation affect air travel symptoms such as throat and eye irritation, headaches, dizziness, and motion sickness.

The studies showed passengers wanted more light and space in the cabin, so Boeing designed 18.5in x 11in (470mm x 280mm) windows which, the company says, are 40% larger than those on other aircraft.

Many of the technologies Boeing was planning to incorporate in the Sonic Cruiser concept were transferred across to the 787 Dreamliner programme. BOEING

> **INITIAL CONSULTATIONS WITH FLIERS REVEALED "THE DEEP PSYCHOLOGICAL NEEDS PEOPLE HAVE WHEN THEY'RE INSIDE AN AIRCRAFT".**
>
> **Blake Emery,** then Director, Differentiation Strategy for Boeing Commercial Airplanes

From the cabin to the cockpit, the Boeing 787 Dreamliner is very different to previous generations of the company's commercial airliners in many ways. **Mark Broadbent** reports

The physical window shades were replaced by an electric dimming switch that lets passengers change the tint of the window, from fully transparent to completely dimmed, and therefore control the light level coming through.

Boeing decided to use LED mood lighting for the cabin to further enhance light and space. Flight attendants can adjust the lights' brightness and colour – there are 128 colour combinations, ranging from oranges and reds to greens and blues – to suit the time of day and the stage of the flight. The overhead baggage bins store up and away rather than cutting into the space above the seats. Economy seats are 18in (457mm) wide (they are larger for premium classes) and there is 26.5in (673mm) between the aisles.

The research also showed passengers wanted a more comfortable ride, so Boeing designed nose-mounted sensors for the 787 that detect turbulence and send messages to the aircraft's control surfaces. Bob Whittington, then Senior Vice-President and Chief Engineer for the 787, explained: "The flight control surfaces actually sense. If you hit a gust of wind in flight, these sensors understand that gust and they will deploy [the control surfaces] in different ways to reduce the effects."

Emery claimed this smoothing out of bumps means the rate at which a 787 moves if it hits turbulence is only 3ft (0.9m), compared with 9ft (2.7m) in other aircraft.

Boeing also focused on reducing cabin noise by developing what it describes as "advanced vibration isolation" in the sidewalls and ceilings, using materials for

MAIN • **Boeing set ambitious goals for the 787. It wanted to produce an aircraft that would burn 20% less fuel, cut operating airlines' costs by 20 to 25%, as well as giving passengers an improved travelling experience.**
LARS VELING

An early artist's impression of Boeing's new mid-sized, twin-engined aircraft, known as the Super Efficient Airliner and dubbed the 7E7, which eventually evolved into the Dreamliner.
BOEING

Part of the manufacturer's work on improving the passenger experience involved fitting LED mood lighting in the cabin that can be adjusted to suit different phases of the flight.
AIRTEAMIMAGES.COM/ PAWARIN PRAPUKDEE

the cabin interior designed to reduce squeaks, and putting serrated chevrons in the engine nacelles to minimise background engine noise.

Up in the Air

The biggest innovations in the interior concern technology related to something that cannot be seen – the cabin air. On its website Boeing claims: "The cabin air in the 787 is cleaner than today's other commercial aircraft." Traditionally, cabin air conditioning uses compressed bleed air from the engines. By contrast, the Dreamliner has inlets on the fuselage that draw fresh air from the outside. Electrically powered compressors push this through air conditioning packs and distribute it throughout the cabin.

As with many other airliners, the 787 has a high-efficiency particulate air (HEPA) filter to remove viruses, bacteria and fungi from the cabin. However, Boeing says its research showed HEPA filters still miss the microscopic molecules of odours, irritants and contaminants (such as cleaning agents and cosmetics) that contribute to throat, eye and nose irritation passengers can experience during a flight. For that reason, the company added an extra gaseous filtration system to remove such molecules from the air and make the 787's cabin fresher.

Another important contributor to the cabin environment is pressurisation. Most airliners are typically pressurised with a cabin altitude of 8,000ft but the 787's is 6,000ft. Research involving more than 500 volunteers aged 21 to 75 in a barometric pressure chamber showed that at a 6,000ft pressurisation altitude, people absorbed 8% more oxygen and experienced less fatigue, dizziness and headaches. A further reduction, to 5,000ft, showed no additional benefit. That suggested 6,000ft was an optimal altitude for passenger comfort. So Boeing pressurised the 787's cabin to that level.

Emery's view is that the key to the Dreamliner's interior is the way this lower cabin altitude, the filters and the fresh air from the outside, all combine through the light coming through the windows, the LED lighting and the anti-turbulence sensors to create a feeling of well-being. He said: "On the 787 there are a couple of things that are easy for the brain to pick out. When you talk with passengers there's certain things they will enumerate; [the] smooth ride, quietness, the big windows. What people don't realise they're reacting to is the way everything plays together."

> "ON ITS WEBSITE BOEING CLAIMS: "THE CABIN AIR IN THE 787 IS CLEANER THAN TODAY'S OTHER COMMERCIAL AIRCRAFT.""

The Importance of Composites

The cabin's look and feel are tangibles for travellers, but innovation in the Dreamliner goes beyond the interior. Indeed, the lower cabin altitude is only possible thanks to the biggest innovation of all in the 787 – the extensive use of carbon fibre composites.

These make up nearly 50% of the aircraft's structure, including the fuselage, tail and wings. Aluminium, historically the material from which most of an airliner is built, makes up only 20%, while titanium parts account for 15%, steel 10%, and other materials 5%.

Achieving the 6,000ft cabin altitude requires a high level of pressurisation. In an airliner made mainly from

Connectivity

Connectivity is an important aspect of airline operations – both for a carrier's operations and for passengers' in-flight experience. The 787 was designed to be future-proofed for these capabilities through what Boeing calls "e-Enabling".

A Boeing spokeswoman explained: "We designed the 787 Family to allow easy retrieval of data and information and for communication to the ground. This includes the onboard architecture and ground interfaces to enable information to come off the aircraft to the back office."

The 787 can transmit real-time data to the ground through local area networks and Wi-Fi connectivity aboard, making it possible for an airline's operations team on the ground to access information about the aircraft during the flight that, previously, they would only have been able to access manually after the aircraft had landed.

There is a lot of information to go at: each Dreamliner flight generates 500Gb worth of data. Boeing says that making all this information about the aircraft directly available to airlines' maintenance operations reduces costs, automates configuration reporting, and enables software parts to be transferred wirelessly and stored.

The benefits aren't limited to airlines. The e-Enabling infrastructure means 787 operators can provide the very latest in-flight entertainment and connectivity (IFE&C) to passengers and accommodate new consumer electronics technology (tablet devices being a prime example) aboard the aircraft. The 787's IFE&C options, the Panasonic eXConnect and Thales TopConnect, are line-fit during production.

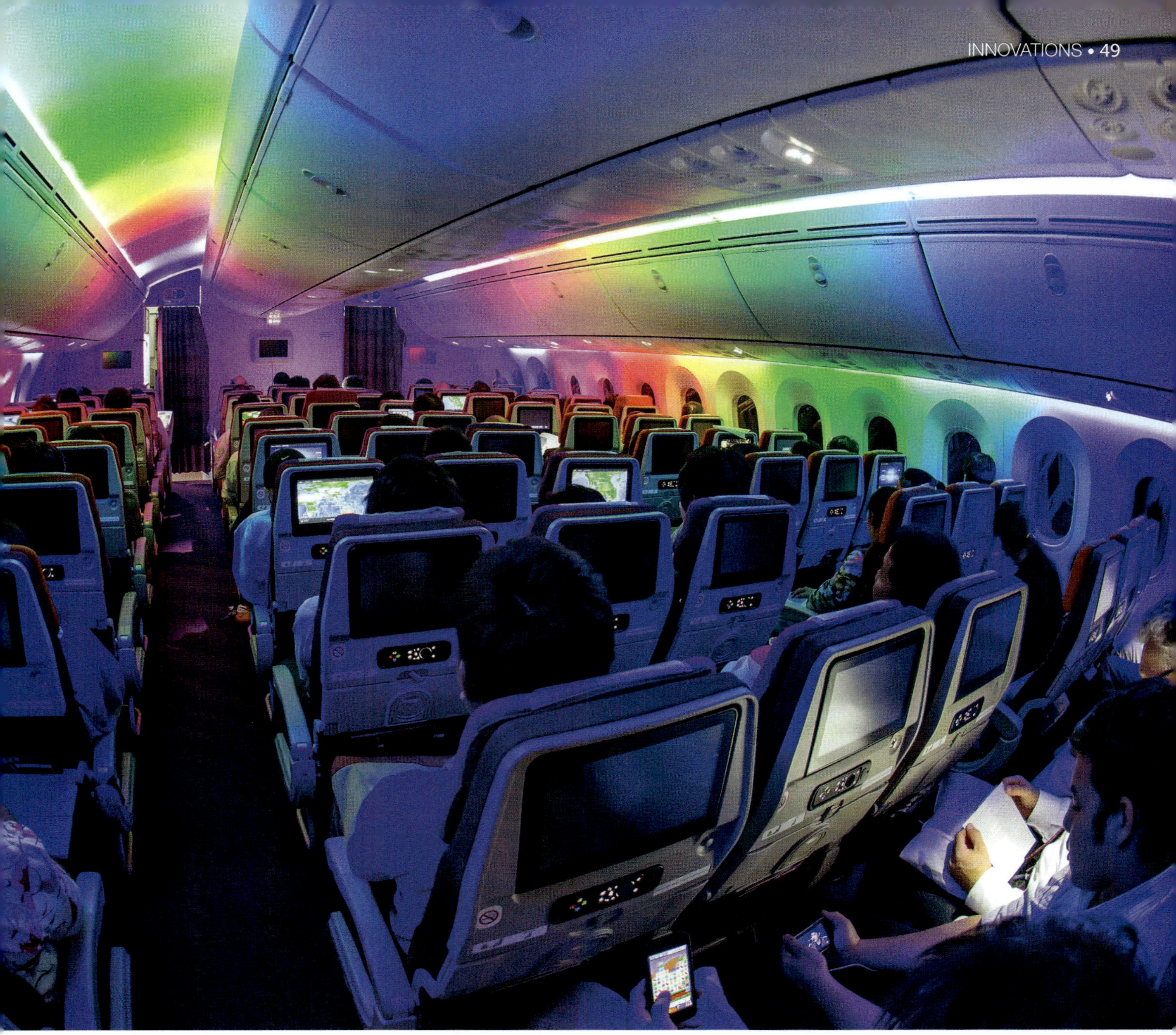

United Airlines has configured its 787 Economy cabin in a nine-abreast layout AIRTEAMIMAGES.COM/ NATHAN ZALEMAN

ABOVE LEFT • The Ethiopian Airlines Business Class cabin uses a 2-2-2 layout. AIRTEAMIMAGES.COM/ EDWIN CHAI

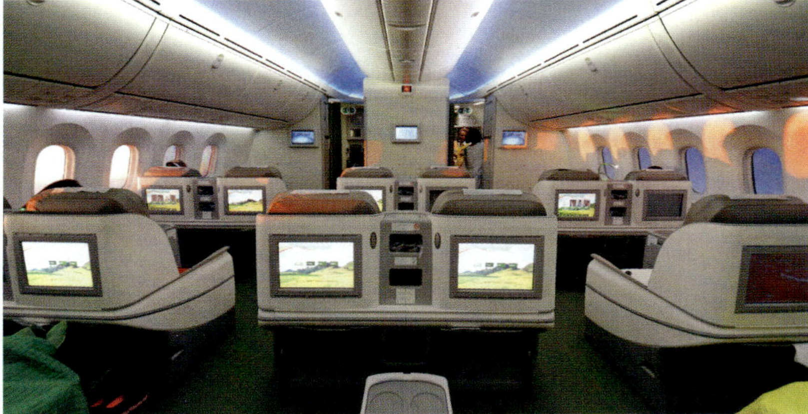

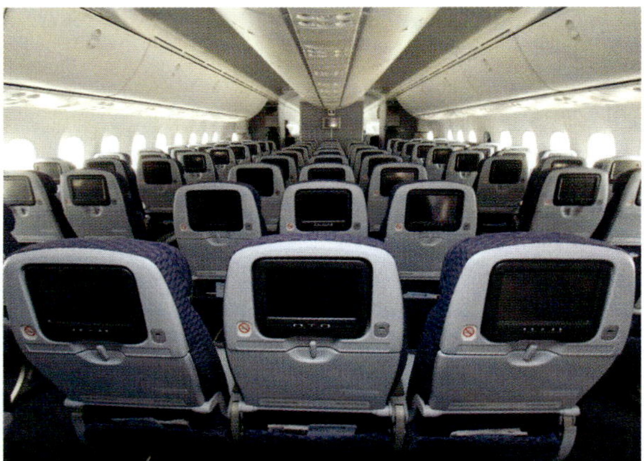

aluminium, this would raise structural fatigue concerns. Boeing says those concerns were minimised in the 787 because materials research, carried out during the aircraft's development, showed that composites offered better fatigue resistance. By using composites for the fuselage, Boeing says it was able to achieve a higher pressurisation and therefore attain the lower cabin altitude from which the research showed passengers benefited.

Composites were used extensively for other reasons. Research showed they were lighter than aluminium, meaning they could contribute substantially towards ensuring the 787 would give airlines a 25% reduction in operating costs from earlier widebodies. A Boeing spokeswoman said composites also need 30% less scheduled maintenance, which increases availability and saves time and money on heavy structural checks.

The Electric Jet

Another key difference in the 787 from other airliners is its predominantly electrical architecture. Historically, high-pressure bleed air diverted from engines is used to power the pneumatic architecture »

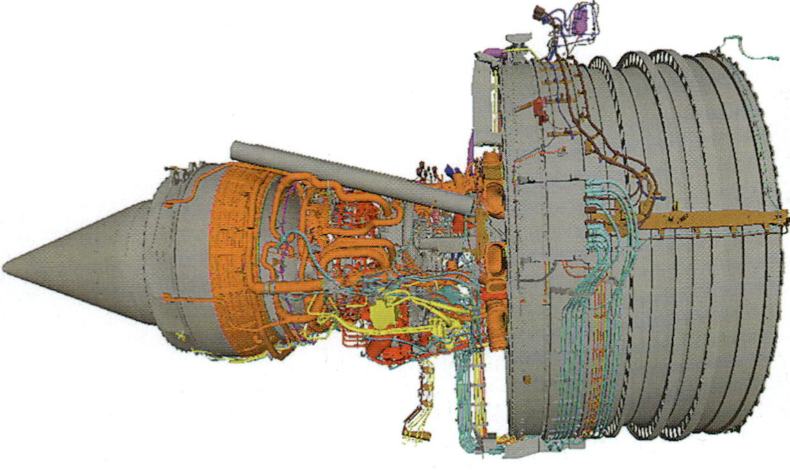

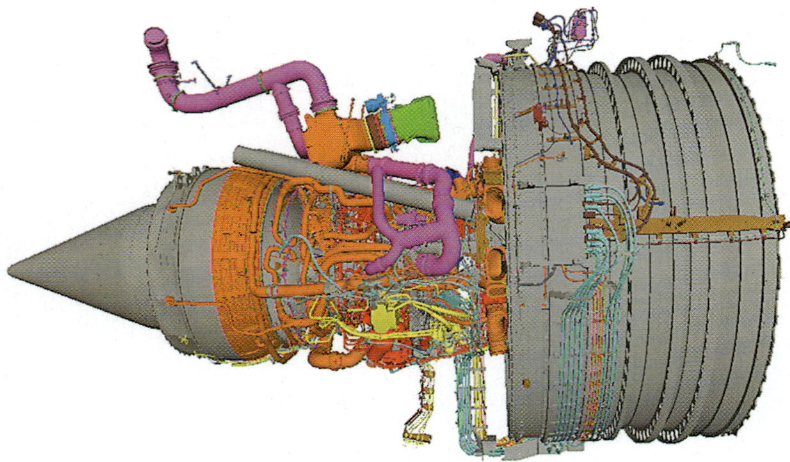

that runs key systems such as the auxiliary power unit starter, hydraulics, wing anti-ice protection, and cabin air conditioning. By contrast, on the 787 these and other systems rely on electrical power. For instance, the wing anti-ice protection is provided by blankets in the leading edges that are heated by the electrical system as required, rather than the established method of ducting hot bleed air into the wings.

Boeing decided to adopt an electrical architecture for several reasons. In its in-house magazine, AERO, the company says the system provides improved fuel economy as the aircraft is lighter from not having the pneumatic systems (and their associated ducts and valves) a traditional system requires. Boeing says the innovation accounts for around 3% of the Dreamliner's fuel savings.

The article states: "The 787's no-bleed systems architecture allows the engines to produce thrust more efficiently – all of the high-speed air produced by the engines goes to thrust. Pneumatic systems that divert high-speed air from the engines rob conventional aircraft of some thrust and increase the engine's fuel consumption."

Further benefits, Boeing says, are reduced maintenance costs due to the elimination of "maintenance-intensive" bleed systems, improved reliability, and more efficient power extraction, transfer and usage.

The architecture has an impact on the 787's flight deck, too, as it means fewer physical units are needed for the flight deck display, communications, navigation and surveillance equipment. Any changes can be made through software upgrades.

Flight Deck

The Dreamliner flight deck's large 15.1in (383mm) multifunction displays, dual head-up displays (HUDs), and dual electronic flight bags (EFBs) mean it looks very different from those of earlier Boeings, and the changes go beyond appearances.

Captain Randy Neville, Chief Pilot for the 787 with Boeing Commercial Airplanes, explained: "Pilots can tailor how they want to present information. We can move information with a single button push to the left or right side of the cockpit. There's a lot of flexibility in moving information around depending on the stage of the flight or which pilot is flying the aircraft."

This aspect of the flight deck was praised by Captain Steve Bull, a training captain with Virgin Atlantic Airways, one of the 787-9's initial operators. He said: "There's one super function called the comm button, where the operator can completely modify it to their own software. On our comm page we have all our load sheet procedures unique to Virgin. It's automatic as well.

"There's another page for reminding crews to do anything from making a [radio] call in half an hour, to making the aircraft climb, to reminding you to wake another crew member from crew rest. It takes [out]

all the things that you used to have to scribble notes down for."

The HUDs are one of the most noticeable differences between the 787's flight deck and those on other Boeings. Capt Neville said: "I'm glad we went down the path of having it as standard equipment. On a precision approach you have to transition from looking at the instruments to actually see the runway. With the HUD, you're already looking outside. It has all of the

> ❝ THE HUDS ARE ONE OF THE MOST NOTICEABLE DIFFERENCES BETWEEN THE 787'S FLIGHT DECK AND THOSE ON OTHER BOEINGS. ❞

standard information you need to fly the aircraft – the airspeed scales, altitude scales, a flight director to tell you where to turn, instrument approach [and] whether you're above a flight path [or] left or right of your course."

Another notable flight deck feature is the electronic checklist. Capt Neville said: "With one button push, the checklist will come up. If it specifies a step in that procedure,

Large multifunction screens, head-up displays and electronic flight bags give the 787's flight deck a very different look to previous Boeing airliners.
AIRTEAMIMAGES.COM/RUDI BOIGELOT

a switch change for instance, it will automatically detect if that switch is in the proper position [and] automatically check off that step. It decreases pilot workload and it's a very nice feature to have all that information available at your fingertips."

Virgin's Capt Bull thinks the checklist is especially useful. He said: "You can never leave anything out in the 787. The safety implications are fabulous; it's always looking after you. You can't line up on a runway without having done the before take-off checks. In conventional aeroplanes you're »

LEFT • Two key features on the 787's flight deck that help enhance the crew's awareness are a vertical situational display – in the lower part of the MFD on the left – and the airport ground moving map (on the right). AIRTEAMIMAGES. COM/FELIX GOTTWOLD

RIGHT • The Boeing 787's cockpit has been designed to have a lot of commonality with the larger 777. This means crews can convert from one type to the other in just a matter of days. LARS VELING

relying on doing your scans and reading [physical] checklists."

Avionics

Dreamliner pilots have at their disposal avionics that haven't previously featured on Boeings. A notable example is the integrated approach navigation (IAN) system that helps pilots conduct required navigation performance procedures.

Capt Neville explained: "With a button push, [the IAN] gives you a smooth, continuous flight path all the way down towards the runway, but it keeps the procedure intuitive. It reduces the workload and keeps very common procedures, regardless of whether it's a precision approach or a non-precision approach."

An enhanced vertical situational display provides a graphic rendering of approaching terrain, and a ground moving map shows a detailed picture of the aircraft's current location on the ground. The former gives a vertical reference of what the aircraft is doing, and according to Capt Bull is, "fantastic for flying precision approaches".

One of the more unusual aspects of the Dreamliner design is how the type's wing curves during flight which is most obvious when viewed head-on.
BOEING

The ground moving map shows individual taxiways and gates, useful for taxiing at airports with complex layouts or in poor visibility.

The 787 has dual Class 3 touchscreen EFBs that provide maps, charts, manuals, onboard maintenance functions, and a document browser. The EFBs also have an onboard performance tool that enables flight and maintenance crews to calculate take-off, landing, weight and balance information.

Capt Bull explained: "Rather than doing [calculations] the old-fashioned way, going into manuals, you input all the information about the take-off and landing, take-off and fuel weights [and] all the key weather at departure. The beauty of it is that it won't ever let you do anything wrong. It will tell you if there's an error, [for example] if you can't lift a certain weight off the runway. You have to go back in and change things, so that's a really clever tool."

Despite all these innovations, Boeing wanted maximum commonality with the 777's flight deck to ensure a common type rating between the two families and therefore give operational savings for airlines flying both types. Some of the 777's flight laws were designed into the 787's flight control system, with displays and switches placed in similar positions to where they are located on the 777 flight deck. Boeing also kept its established wheel-and-column control layout.

An Efficient Cruiser

Boeing's desire to provide big operational savings for airlines with the 787 has led to other innovations. Some of the most important of these concern the Dreamliner's aerodynamics. As with a glider, the 787 has high aspect ratio wings (aspect ratio being the width of the wing against its span), which together with the raked wing tips is designed

> **AS WITH A GLIDER, THE 787 HAS HIGH ASPECT RATIO WINGS (ASPECT RATIO BEING THE WIDTH OF THE WING AGAINST ITS SPAN),**

The Wing Curve

One of the most commented-upon features of the 787 is the curve in the aircraft's wings, which is seen most visibly when looking at the Dreamliner head-on as it takes off. So why does the aircraft have this very distinctive feature? It's all to do with aerodynamics, explained Bob Whittington, then Vice-President and Chief Engineer for the 787.

He said: "A wing is a very complicated set of compromises. You want a very thin wing to increase speed. You have to trade off the angle that the wings sweep back, the thickness of the wing and the shape of the wing. We wanted to maintain a Mach 0.85 speed.

"The composites enabled us to design a wing with great aspect ratio and still thin enough to get a Mach 0.85 aircraft. The outcome of that thin wing with the large aspect ratio and the unique shape of the wing tips generate that curve you see when you take off."

to maximise aerodynamic lift and help the aircraft fly as efficiently as possible.

Whittington said: "The wing changes shape during flight. In different points in the flight you get a different combination of spoilers, flaps [and] ailerons that change the shape of the wing to move the loading profile around to optimise for the least amount of drag and the highest speed."

There are other seemingly small, though significant, innovations that contribute to the aerodynamics. The wing trailing edges have pivot flaps that, Boeing says, help improve lift-to-drag characteristics and reduce weight and maintenance burdens. The 787-9 (though not the -8) also has hybrid laminar flow control on the horizontal and vertical tailplanes to reduce drag around the rear of the aircraft.

Whether it is aspects of the aircraft like these that help an airline fly more efficiently, or the big changes such as composites, the new generation of engines, or the features inside the cabin, the 787 has undeniably brought many innovations to the widebody airliner world.

TOP • *Raked wingtips, as demonstrated on this KLM Royal Dutch Airlines 787-9, help to increase the wing's aspect ratio as well as providing increased lift.* AIRTEAMIMAGES.COM/ JEFFREY SCHAFER

ABOVE • *As with a glider, the 787's high aspect ratio wings are designed to maximise aerodynamic lift and help the aircraft fly as efficiently as possible.* BOEING

KLM Royal Dutch Airlines' first Boeing 787-9, PH-HBC (c/n 38760) 'Zonnebloem' (Sunflower), taxies towards the runway at Amsterdam/Schiphol ahead of a crew familiarisation flight. *LARS VELING*

Entry into Service

After many false starts Boeing was finally able to hand over the first production 787 to launch customer All Nippon Airways on September 26, 2011. BOEING

Japan Airlines President Yoshiharu Ueki (left) and Boeing Commercial Airplanes President and CEO Jim Albaugh cutting the ribbon at a delivery ceremony for the carrier's first two 787-8s on March 25, 2012. BOEING

"Today we have the honour of being part of aviation history," proclaimed All Nippon Airway's (ANA) President and CEO Shinichiro Ito after accepting the 'key' to the first production Boeing 787-8. Standing before more than 500 Dreamliner workers, invited guests, airline and Boeing representatives at a rain-soaked ceremony beside the Everett production facility, Boeing Commercial Airplanes President and CEO Jim Albaugh had presented the key with the comment: "Please take very good care of it, we're so proud!"

Boeing had overcome a series of disparate challenges to reach the historic public handover of its first Dreamliner to launch customer ANA on September 26, 2011. Quoted in a Boeing press release, Ito said: "We are delighted to be taking delivery finally of our first 787," his choice of the word 'finally' summing up the airframe, labour force and production woes that had blighted the programme and caused a three-year delivery delay.

The companies had actually completed contractual handover the day before, and on the 27th an ANA crew piloted the 787-liveried jet on its

ferry flight from Paine Field to Tokyo/Haneda Airport. Japan's weather also failed to grace the much-anticipated event with favour, blustery conditions greeting JA801A (c/n 34488) as it landed and then taxied in to an enthusiastic welcome from the airline's personnel. The weather may have been an ominous warning of the storms that lay ahead...

Battery Issues

On October 27, ANA flew the world's first revenue-earning 787 service, albeit the paying passengers on the Tokyo Narita to Hong Kong trip had bought tickets in an online charity auction, while the majority of those on board were airline executives, guests and journalists.

Commercial services started proper on November 1, the two 787s by then in ANA's hands initially operating the Haneda-Okayama and Haneda-Hiroshima routes. By the time Japan Airlines took its first 787 to become the second Dreamliner operator on March 25, 2012, ANA already had five jets in

When Boeing delivered the first customer Dreamliner in September 2011, there must have been a collective sigh of relief among company executives. Of course the high-tech machine was expected to have teething problems, but a series of high-profile battery failures led to a dramatic three-month grounding, as **Paul E Eden** reports.

The failed battery unit from the JAL 787 that caught fire at Boston/Logan on January 7, 2013, leading to the grounding of the entire fleet. NTSB

The JAL 787-8, JA829J (c/n 34839), was repaired and returned to service. AIRTEAMIMAGES.COM/KSK

service and Boeing had discovered a problem in the fuselage structure of some aircraft that required rectification.

Ethiopian Airlines became the third 787 carrier on August 14, less than a month after ANA had reported that the Rolls-Royce Trent 1000s on five of its aircraft required unscheduled fixes. Further engine glitches and then a hydraulic issue affected the fleet, but teething problems are common for new aircraft, especially those that push the boundaries of technology,

and there seemed to be no particular drama.

In December the FAA ordered inspections of all Dreamliners after fuel leaks were reported, but worse was still to come. On January 7, 2013, fire erupted aboard an empty JAL 787 parked at Logan International Airport, Boston. Although the incident was controlled within 40 minutes, the media eye was still focused on the Dreamliner, JAL and Boston when the airline suffered another 787 fuel »

leak and cancelled a flight out of Logan International the next day.

On the 9th, United Airlines announced that it had discovered wiring issues around the main batteries on six of its Dreamliners and with suspicion already falling on the battery installation after the Logan fire, the US National Transportation Safety Board (NTSB) began an investigation. Meanwhile, two more JAL fuel leaks led the Japanese aviation authorities to begin a separate enquiry.

The dream quickly became a nightmare on January 16, when an ANA jet flying between Ube and Tokyo made an emergency landing at Takamatsu after repeated battery warnings accompanied by fumes in the cockpit. A battery fire was found to be the cause and after JAL suffered a second battery-related incident at Boston, the Federal Aviation Administration moved to enact a decision it had not made against a US-built airliner since the DC-10 of 1979 – it grounded the entire Dreamliner fleet.

Battery Team

With deliveries halted but production continuing, Boeing assigned a dedicated battery team to the issue, while authorities in Japan and the US attempted to define the cause of the failures. Pinpointing an exact source of the fires ultimately proved impossible, but faulty wiring or problems within individual battery cells seem most likely to have generated short circuits, leading to overheating that caused runaway thermal events across cells. Boeing created a robust defence against the potential effects of cell failure, based on a system of layered protection.

Under lights: The first Boeing 787-8 is prepared for handover to launch customer ANA.
BOEING

Ethiopian Airlines became the third customer – and the first African carrier – to take delivery of a Dreamliner when ET-AOQ (c/n 34745) joined its fleet on August 14, 2012.
BOEING

The Dreamliner's batteries are housed in bays in the lower forward and lower centre fuselage areas. In the original design, groups of lithium-ion batteries, each comprising eight individual cells contained within an aluminium box, were located in each bay.

After the remedial effort, each cell is now wrapped in insulating tape as a first-layer defence against thermal runaway. A set of insulating dividers then creates a physical barrier between cells, and the revised assembly is returned to the aluminium box, which is now encased in a 1/8in (3mm) thick steel container.

A vent system in the cells, dividers, aluminium box and steel case ensures that smoke, fumes and fluids that might result from a battery failure exhaust from the unit, where Titanium pipes lead them to external ports; these vent overboard, rather than being released into the aircraft. The result is essentially the

> **" BOEING CREATED A ROBUST DEFENCE AGAINST THE POTENTIAL EFFECTS OF CELL FAILURE, BASED ON A SYSTEM OF LAYERED PROTECTION. "**

same battery but in a fireproof vented case, the whole package weighing 150lb (68kg) compared with 63lb (29kg) for the original unit.

With trials completed and approvals received airlines, with the help of Boeing engineers, started to incorporate the modifications – the first revenue-earning Dreamliner services restarting again on April 26, 2013. The NTSB's report into the lithium-ion battery fire on the JAL 787 at Boston/Logan issued on December 1, 2014, criticised Boeing and its battery supplier Yuasa, while it also said the FAA lacked sufficient oversight. The board's report added that the US manufacturer and the FAA failed to recognise the potential for a so-called thermal runaway event and therefore did not require its engineers to perform thermal runaway tests as part of the certification process.

The three-month grounding caused huge problems for Boeing at the time, however modified 787s were quickly returned to scheduled operations, enabling the manufacturer to concentrate on ramping up production as well as developing the next two members of the Dreamliner Family, the -9 and -10.

THE DESTINATION FOR
AVIATION ENTHUSIASTS
Visit us today and discover all our latest releases

Order from our online shop...
shop.keypublishing.com/specials
Call +44 (0)1780 480404 *(Monday to Friday 9am - 5.30pm GMT)*
Free 2nd class P&P on BFPO orders. Overseas charges apply.

869/25

Ethiopian Airlines became the first African operator of the Boeing 787-8 Dreamliner when it took delivery of its initial example on August 14, 2012.
AIRTEAMIMAGES.COM/ YOCHAI

Etihad Airways operated its inaugural 787-9 service between Abu Dhabi and Düsseldorf on February 1, 2015. The United Arab Emirates' flag carrier celebrated the introduction of the new type with a striking new "Facets of Abu Dhabi" livery.
AIRTEAMIMAGES.COM/ DIPANKAR BHAKTA

Kenya Airways took delivery of its ninth Dreamliner – 5Y-KZJ (c/n 36046) – on October 29, 2015. This aircraft is being operated on lease from BOC Aviation.
AIRTEAMIMAGES.COM/ SERGE BAILLEUL

Oman Air currently operates two 787-8s and seven 787-9s which serve multiple destinations from Muscat-Seeb International Airport.
AIRTEAMIMAGES.COM/ DIPANKAR BHAKTA

Qatar Airways is one of the fastest growing airlines in the world and operates 51 Boeing 787 Dreamliners with an astonishing 130 more on order, announced in May 2025. It took delivery of its first example on October 5, 2012.
AIRTEAMIMAGES.COM/ PHILIPPE NORET

Royal Air Maroc joined the Dreamliner family in December 2014 and now operates the type on services from Casablanca to Paris/ Orly and New York/ John F Kennedy International Airports. In 2024, it announced new 787 services from Casablanca to Toronto and Montreal, additions in the US to Miami and Washington, as well as new regular services to Sao Paulo (Brazil) and Beijing.
AIRTEAMIMAGES.COM/ MATHIEU POULIOT

Saudia, the flag carrier of Saudi Arabia, took simultaneous delivery of two 787-9s, HZ-ARA (c/n 41544) and HZ-ARB (c/n 41545), on February 2, 2016. The carrier currently operates 13 787-8s and eight 787-10s. In March 2023, Boeing announced that Saudia had ordered up to 49 further Dreamliners.
BOEING

The 787 was a key element of Royal Jordanian Airlines' fleet modernisation programme that has seen the carrier retire its Airbus A340-200s and return its A330-200s to their lessors.
AIRTEAMIMAGES.COM/ MATHIEU POULIOT

From the
Flight Deck

Former Boeing Chief Test Pilot Captain **Frank Santoni** describes what it was like to be involved in the 787 Dreamliner's flight test programme.

"To put the Boeing 787-8 into context from a flying perspective, it is about the same size as a 767 but has a slightly bigger fuselage and cabin, and is a little longer. It has more range – almost as much as the 777-200 – with engines in the 66,000lb-thrust class. The Dash 9 is a little bigger again, with even more range.

"When we designed the initial version of the 777, in 1994, it had a gross weight of about 506,000lb [229,518kg]. Since then the aircraft has grown to 775,000lb [351,534kg], using essentially the same wing, and is a little larger, but generally keeps faith to the original design.

"So you might wonder why we built an aeroplane back in the early 1990s that we'd have to keep refining and making bigger. Analysing the 777's development process raised an important question for the Boeing design team: why did it take so long to

The Boeing 787-8 flight test programme involved six aircraft – ZA001 through to ZA006 – four examples flew with Rolls-Royce Trent 1000 engines and two were powered by General Electric GEnx-1Bs. The FAA and EASA jointly certified the 787 on August 26, 2011; first deliveries followed shortly afterwards.
ALL IMAGES BOEING

OPPOSITE • Air-to-air with the first Boeing 787-8 during its maiden flight on December 15, 2009. The aircraft, accompanied by a T-33 chase plane, flew for around three hours before landing back at Paine Field, Everett.

reach the type's optimum design, the -300ER, some 12 years later?

"So, moving forward to the next generation of widebody airliners, why don't we start with an airframe with an optimum design from the start? We believe the 787 has that and therefore doesn't have a lot of growth in it. You get a lot more performance out of the engines, the new wing and the use of composites.

"Put them all together [and] you get about a 20% improvement over the aircraft the Dreamliner is replacing. It's a completely different model of how we build our aeroplanes.

"When I sit in the cockpit of the Dreamliner, I ask every pilot I'm flying with the same question. What are the first two things that strike you about this cockpit? We have dual head-up displays [HUDs] – just like the fighter guys use – that project images from the primary flight instruments superimposed on a piece of glass that sits in front of the pilot.

"You can look at them, and through them you can see the real world outside the cockpit. The dual head-up displays are standard. If you buy this aeroplane you get them, if you want to take them off we'll charge you! There are certain customers that don't like that answer, but that's the way it is.

"The second thing that attracts the attention of the pilots is the size of the windows. I swear new pilots just sit there and look out and go 'wow'!

"The Dreamliner has the most advanced fly-by-wire system ever developed for a commercial aeroplane. For instance, conventionally when you roll the wheel, you're making the aeroplane roll by moving ailerons and spoilers on the wings. In this aeroplane, when you move the control wheel you're actually controlling the roll rate, telling the computer 'I want to roll at a certain rate' – a slight difference to previous generation jets.

"In a conventional aeroplane, when you kick the rudder, you're moving the rudder pedals via hydraulics or direct linkage. In the Dreamliner, when you move the rudder pedals, you're commanding left or right sideslip. If you don't touch the rudder pedals you're commanding the aeroplane to zero sideslip, and if something happens, like you lose an engine, it will still maintain zero sideslip and engage the rudder for you automatically."

Describing the capabilities of the 787s new fly-by-wire control system, Captain Santoni demonstrated a particularly interesting test they put the aircraft through – the minimum control speed in the air. "What we do is put the aeroplane at full thrust in a good climb and a typical configuration such as when we are flying a go-around.

"Full thrust, 20 degrees pitched up, then we shut down one of the engines, asking the pilot in command to control the aeroplane to within 20 degrees of the initial heading.

"So that's 66,000lb of thrust from one engine and zero from the other. The fly-by-wire computers immediately kick in and keep the aircraft flying along its initial track with very little deviation. We've even demonstrated this with hands and feet fully off the controls to see what the aircraft does and there is very little change to the flight profile. The system is pretty incredible stuff and is a valuable contribution to flight safety."

Another interesting demonstration of the aeroplane's capabilities is >>

landing the jet in high-crosswind conditions. Santoni explained that Boeing flew one of the prototype aircraft to Iceland, a favoured place for trials as it's often windy there and the airport at Keflavik has two runways at 90 degrees to each other.

"We flew in crosswind conditions of around 25kts, gusting to 32 there, which proved to be well within the aircraft's capabilities. When flying a crosswind approach, the question is what window do you look out of? The answer is the side window. The aeroplane is very forgiving in crosswinds and gusts."

Describing the process of checking the aircraft's brakes, he said: "As soon as you touch down you hit the brakes as hard as you can and bring the jet to a stop. This can be achieved in as little as 2,000ft [610m] and we also put a little rubber down on the runway.

"However, the trick here is to take off again really quickly so that you don't blow the fuse plug [on the tyres to prevent overheating].

"Another test that really gets our test pilots' attention is where you apply the brakes to full before touching down. It's really hard to do – and pilots hate doing it – but it's necessary to check the inner skid actuator releases; and you don't blow all the tyres!"

Among other "exciting" tests for pilots, Santoni

The fifth Boeing 787-8 prototype to fly, ZA005, N787FT (c/n 40694), was the first to be powered by General Electric GEnx engines.

Boeing's fourth 787-8 prototype, N7874 (c/n 40693), arrives at Colorado Springs Airport in May 2010 for a short series of high-elevation flight tests. General Electric GEnx engines.

explained, is the maximum energy brake test. "The aircraft is filled to its maximum weight using water as ballast, then the speed needed before applying full brakes to get maximum energy is calculated, this is without deploying the engine thrust reversers.

"During the test the aircraft will taxi for about four miles, making several stops to get some heat into the brakes, before lining up on the runway. After a short countdown the engines are spooled up to full power, brakes are released and the jet accelerates quickly down the runway. When it hits the pre-defined cut speed point, full brakes are applied: Then it's just a case of hanging on! The test is over in just

BELOW • *The second Dreamliner variant, the stretched -9, takes off on its maiden flight from Paine Field on September 18, 2013.*

half a second. If the aircraft doesn't hit the speed right it doesn't get to maximum energy; hit it too late and you'll end up off the end of the runway. This is a pretty critical test.

"Accelerating down the runway, you'll see the nose dip when the pilot applies the brakes, at the right cut speed – about 185kts. The brakes will actually start to glow: they're carbon fibre and they almost turn to glass.

"When the aircraft finally comes to a stop, there's a small fire – it's usually dust or grease that comes out of some of the fittings. The brakes are deliberately pre-worn for the test, because in service you could have a maximum brake situation when they are nearly ready for changing.

"Overall our goal was to achieve a common type rating for both the 777 and 787; it's really good for the customer because it makes the training courses a lot shorter and makes for more efficiency.

"So 90% of the normal procedures on the Dreamliner are the same as those for 777. The normal checklists used before take-off and landing are identical.

"The procedures in the checklist that you would use from memory – and those that, if you had a major emergency happen to the aeroplane, you had to do from memory – are also identical. The ones you don't have to do by memory are almost the same, but those you read anyhow.

"The way you fly this aeroplane is also the same. All the processes and actions – such as putting the gear down, extending or retracting the flaps, taxiing – are all exactly the same. This results in 777 pilots having to attend just a five-day conversion course to enable them to fly the Dreamliner."

Jetstar Airways has taken delivery of 11 787-8s originally ordered by parent Qantas.
AIRTEAMIMAGES.COM/ DIPANKAR BHAKTA

After launching services with the Boeing 777, low-cost long-haul carrier Scoot has now switched to the Dreamliner. The Singapore Airlines' subsidiary currently operates 10 787-8s and 10 787-9s.
SETH JAWORSKI

Japan Airlines (JAL) became the second carrier to take delivery of the Boeing 787-8 after rival All Nippon Airlines. The first aircraft, JA821J (c/n 34832), was handed over on March 25, 2012. After conducting crew familiarisation flights, the type was used to launch a new non-stop service from Tokyo to Boston on April 22.
AIRTEAMIMAGES.COM/ SIMON GREGORY

The first Boeing 787-8 from the manufacturer's second Dreamliner final assembly line in North Charleston, South Carolina was delivered to Air India. The aircraft, VT-ANI (c/n 35277), was handed over on October 5, 2012.
AIRTEAMIMAGES.COM/ OLIVIER CORNELOUP

The launch customer for the Dreamliner, All Nippon Airlines (ANA) remained patient throughout the type's long development cycle. It received its first example, JA801A (c/n 34488), on September 25, 2011. AIRTEAMIMAGES.COM/TT

Air New Zealand greatly benefitted from Boeing 787 Family's 330-minute ETOPS approval. This allows the aircraft to operate up to five and a half hours single-engine flying time away from the nearest suitable diversionary airport. AIRTEAMIMAGES.COM/DIPANKAR BHAKTA

Prior to its delivery to Vietnam Airlines, Boeing displayed 787-9, VN-A361 (c/n 35151), at the 2015 Paris Airshow. The jet was put through a spectacular daily flight demonstration by the company's test pilots. AIRTEAMIMAGES.COM/ PHILIPPE NORET

Thai Airways International signed lease agreements with Netherlands-based lessor AerCap and currently operates six 787-8s and two 787-9s. In 2024, it announced a further 45 orders of the aircraft. AIRTEAMIMAGES.COM/ ANDRE NORDEIM

The arrival of its 787-8 Dreamliners enabled Chinese carrier Xiamen Airlines to launch its first intercontinental service - to Amsterdam/Schiphol - in July 2015. AIRTEAMIMAGES.COM/ WEIMENG

Training the Pilots

Today's highly competitive commercial aviation sector demands that airlines operate at maximum efficiency. This has led Boeing to develop innovative training solutions for the 787 Dreamliner programme, as **Barry Woods-Turner** discovers.

Even before the first Boeing 787-8 entered scheduled service with All Nippon Airways on November 1, 2011, the US manufacturer had invested significant sums of money in developing state-of-the-art training to prepare cockpit and cabin crews, and maintenance technicians to be ready for the aircraft's arrival. The company's Support and Services Division has a global network of 15 campuses on six continents, supporting more than 80 full-flight simulators as well as a number of advanced-technology 787 training suites.

One of these campuses is located in Crawley, Sussex, close to Gatwick Airport, and was one of the first to receive and commission a 787 Dreamliner training suite. The facility is Boeing's European training hub, employing around 60 staff and operating seven Full Flight Simulators (FFS) including a 737 Classic, 737NG, 757, 767, 777, 787, as well as an Airbus A320.

The potential for the training market is huge, the company's latest Commercial Market Outlook for 2021-2040 predicts the world's airlines will require up to 43,600 aircraft worth an estimated US$7.2 trillion (including 7,670 widebody jets), a major component cost of an overall services market value estimated at US$9.54 trillion. Introducing so many new aircraft into service will create an associated requirement for trained flight-deck crews and maintenance technicians. In its Pilot and Technical Outlook for 2021-2040, given an uneven global recovery from the coronavirus pandemic, the company forecasts the aviation industry will need to supply more than two million additional personnel, including 612,000 commercial airline pilots and 626,000 maintenance technicians.

Boeing has invested significant sums of money – thought to be several hundred million dollars – in the Crawley campus in creating its Dreamliner training suite. The money has been spent not only on the facilities themselves, but also innovative equipment, instructors and courseware and is a fundamental change in how Boeing has organised its customer training. The company says that it is "ensuring that airlines have what they need, when they need it and where they need it".

Inside the 787 full-flight simulator, produced by Thales, there is a dual head-up display system and electronic flight bags.

OPPOSITE BOTTOM •
Capt Masayuki Ishii, ANA Director, 787 Flight Training (left), and Capt Hideaki Hayakawa, ANA Deputy Director, 787 Flight Training, prepare for a training session in the 787 full-flight simulator.

The high-fidelity 787 FFS located at Boeing's Crawley, Sussex campus, enables pilots to become proficient in visual manoeuvres and non-normal procedures such as those affecting the aircraft's handling characteristics.

Fundamental Changes

As the 787 Dreamliner is unlike any airliner programme Boeing has developed before, the company has had to completely rethink its training philosophy. The most obvious difference is that the training is now being taken to the customer, the complete opposite of how it has been done in the past. The last all-new airliner programme launched by Boeing in December 1989, the 777, required that all instruction was carried out at a single location, Seattle on the US West Coast. With Dreamliner training suites now located at strategic points across the globe, Boeing says it remains flexible and, depending on demand, may add to its network.

Boeing has an innovative approach to managing training requirements, which includes the introduction of a points system. Points are allocated against the number of aircraft ordered, so the more jets purchased, the more training points an airline accrues. These are then traded in against a menu of courses covering flight-deck, cabin crew and maintenance programmes that best suits the customer's requirements. Boeing works closely with each customer to ensure the points are used in the most effective way to enable airlines to get the best return for their investment.

Boeing believes it has developed efficient, effective and environmentally progressive training solutions. It is interesting to note that all the Dreamliner courses have been developed electronically to enable cockpit crews and maintainers to transition seamlessly to paperless working. Gone are the days of heavy manuals and thick binders that had to be lugged around. Students are issued with a backpack containing a PC tablet and a USB flash drive that holds all the materials and data they need to complete their course. Now all the information is accessed digitally through search   »

engines thus saving time and effort. But this is just the tip of the training iceberg. Boeing has also invested large sums in modern classrooms and computer simulations that give real-time access to the aircraft and its systems.

The Hardware

Boeing has installed some impressive new teaching hardware at its Crawley campus. On the Dreamliner training solutions programme, Boeing has teamed with French electronics and systems solutions supplier Thales, which in turn has been responsible for the building of most of the computer-based equipment. Much of this was developed concurrently with the real aeroplane. The facility employs four principal training aids for teaching its syllabus:

• **Desk Top Trainers (DTT)** - these are used for the first phase of training where students build up the required knowledge of the aircraft and its systems. The computer programmes use around 98% of the same software that the students will use on the real aircraft, so it is realistic. There are 16 workstations, complete with docking stations for tablet PCs in a classroom used for training pilots and first officers. Each workstation has been built to resemble the cockpit of the 787 and can seat two students. A second room, which is used to train maintenance technicians, is arranged in a lecture-theatre style with a large screen on the front wall with a series of workstations arranged towards the back. Here the use of real-time simulation enables

The advanced 787 full-flight simulator during a training flight. As the aircraft turns onto final approach the crew can rely on information shown on their head-up displays enabling them to keep looking out of the window.

students to practice using the same tools as they would on the real aeroplane. The training is enhanced by using a 3-D virtual aeroplane and active schematics so people can walk around virtually and operate key functions such as opening doors, climbing into equipment bays and replacing parts, just as they would on the real aircraft.

• **Flight Training Device (FTD)** - three 787-9 training systems provide cockpit crews with the same flight management and control systems as the full-flight simulator (FFS), but don't move. They makes an ideal platform for instrument familiarisation and reinforcing knowledge of the aircraft and its systems. They are used to help students become confident with and proficient in normal procedures. The FTDs also simulate the use of electronic flight bags and head-up displays that students will encounter on the FFS and the real aeroplane.

• **Full Flight Simulator (FFS)** – four 787-9 FFS each with six degrees of freedom, which means they have the capacity to go up and down, left to right, forward and backwards and can simulate any time of the day and night as well as different weather scenarios. They include dual head-up displays and electronic flight bags, once again promoting the paperless environment that Boeing has developed for the Dreamliner. The simulators are designed to train pilots to become proficient in visual manoeuvres, instrument landing systems (ILS) and

non-ILS approaches, missed approaches as well as non-normal procedures with emphasis on those affecting handling characteristics, such as how to deal with wind shear and rejected take-offs.

• **Door Trainer** – Boeing also runs a two-day cabin safety course for qualified cabin crew comprising three components – computer-based training (CBT), a visit to a real aeroplane and door tuition. The five-part CBT covers topics such as communications, water, waste and lavatories, emergency doors and special features on the aircraft. The visit to the aeroplane enables students to gain hands-on experience of what they have already learnt. The door training session is for all crew members, including pilots, where instruction is given on how to operate the doors under normal and emergency situations. The door trainer can simulate a number of emergency scenarios, including a ditching on water and an external fire.

Other Options

While some airlines rely upon Boeing's training options, other carriers prefer to train their own cockpit and cabin crews and have invested heavily in providing airline-specific solutions. However, the US manufacturer thought about the needs of airlines right from the start of the 787's development. Boeing has designed the Dreamliner's cockpit to be similar to that of the larger 777, enabling pilots to be jointly certified to fly both types. Commercial airline pilots have traditionally been certified to fly just a

The 787 flight training device (FTD) replicates the management and control systems of a real aeroplane.

Both flight deck and cabin crews have to undergo the mandatory cabin door training session before they are allowed to fly on a commercial passenger service.

The Cabin Safety Training course runs for two days and comprises three key components – computer-based learning, a visit to a real aeroplane for 'hands on' experience and door operation tuition.

single aircraft type and transferring to another would normally take several months of costly additional training.

Converting from the 777 still involves a period of classroom work to understand the new systems and technology used on the Dreamliner, as well as more hands-on simulator training to fully comprehend the aircraft's operating features. However, this additional training takes just over a week to complete and pilots become type certified following two supervised flights in control of the real aeroplane.

A good example of this process is KLM Royal Dutch Airlines, which took delivery of its first 787-9 on December 9, 2015. The national carrier has transferred a number of its most experienced 777 pilots to its Dreamliner operations. The 787 conversion course consists of several days' theory training followed by an exam and four 3.5hr sessions in the simulator with an instructor.

During these sessions, pilots are able to assess how the aeroplane flies as well as practising some of the more critical manoeuvres, such as an engine failure on take-off, loss of cabin pressure at high altitude and handling the aircraft in extreme weather conditions. All this is condensed into an intense week and is followed by two supervised flights on a 787. Prior to launching service with the new type, a group of KLM pilots were given the opportunity to fly a Dreamliner in service through an arrangement with TUI Airlines Netherlands giving them a valuable insight into how the airliner flies.

Whichever training solution an airline elects to use, the arrival of a new aircraft type to the fleet is always an exciting time. As more and more pilots are trained on the 787, Boeing continues to refine its training courses to meet the needs of its customers. The huge investment the US manufacturer has made in its state-of-the-art training solutions will, the company hopes, pay dividends in the future with potential returns that will surely prove that it has invested wisely.

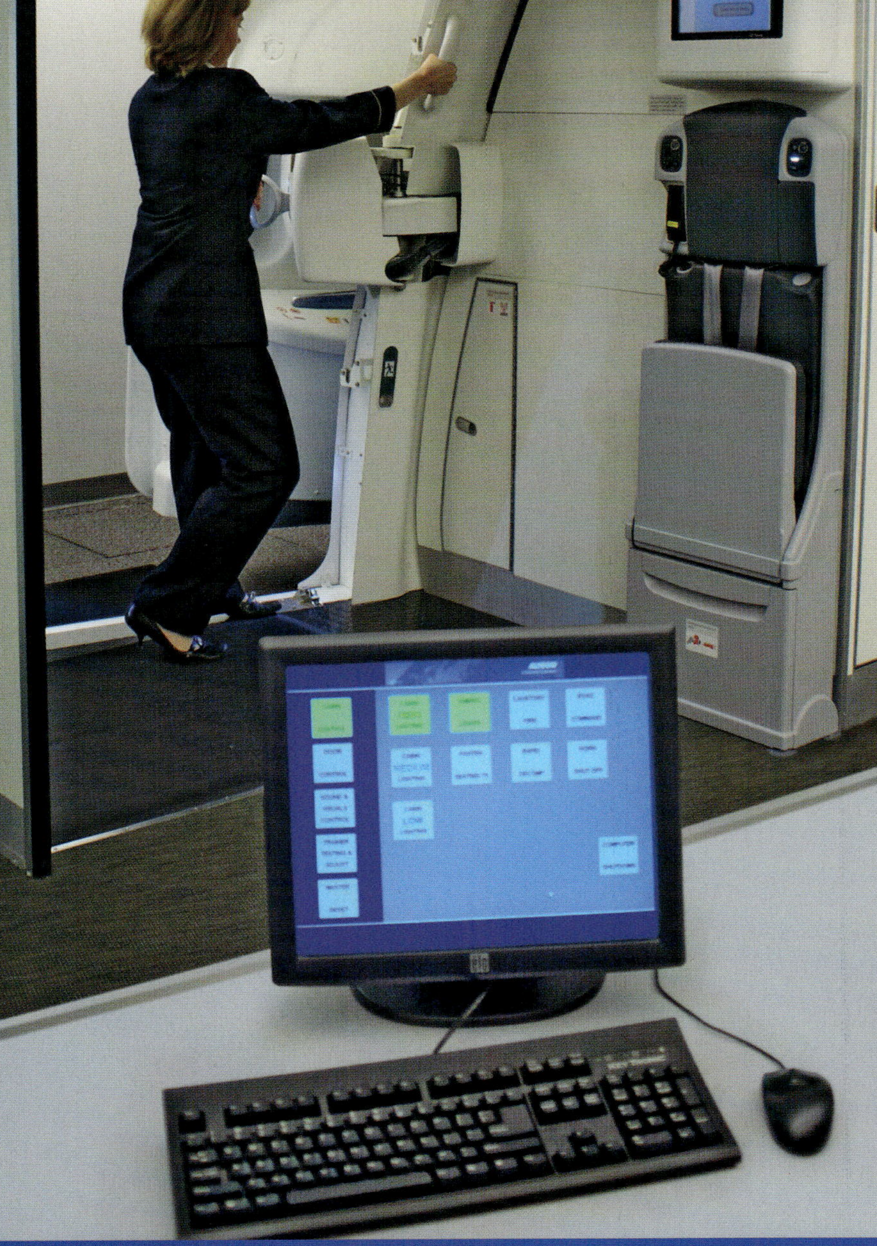

Aeroméxico has eight Boeing 787-8s and 13 787-9s in service.
AIRTEAMIMAGES.COM/ STEVE FLINT

Plan view of American Airlines' Boeing 787-8, N807AA (c/n 40625), as it flares for landing at Los Angeles International Airport.
AIRTEAMIMAGES.COM/TEK

Air Canada received its first Boeing 787-8, C-GHPQ (c/n 35257), on May 18, 2014. The national carrier operates 39 Dreamliners – consisting of eight 787-8s and 31 787-9s – which were delivered through to April 2019.
AIRTEAMIMAGES.COM/ NOAM M

United Airlines became the first North American carrier to operate Boeing's revolutionary new airliner when it took delivery of 787-8, N20904 (c/n 34824), on September 9, 2012. The carrier's first stretched -9 aircraft, N38950 (c/n 36401), arrived two years later.
AIRTEAMIMAGES.COM/
DARREN HOWLE

Colombian flag carrier Avianca received the first Boeing 787-8 from an order for 15 on December 17, 2014. As of May 2025, the carrier operates 16 examples
AIRTEAMIMAGES.COM/
JORGE GUARDIA AGUILA

LAN Airlines (now part of the LATAM Airlines Group operating as LATAM Airlines Chile) was the launch customer for the Boeing 787 in the Americas. The carrier currently operates 37 examples, consisting of ten 787-8s and 27 787-9s. Up to 15 more are on order as of May 2025.
AIRTEAMIMAGES.COM/
ANDRE NORDHEIM

Maintaining
the Dreamliner

Boeing has ushered in new levels of reliability with its 787 – **Ian Goold** examines how this translates across to the maintenance requirements for the type.

ANA completed the first maintenance training class for the 787 Dreamliner nearly 18 months before it took delivery of its initial aircraft. The course was attended by ten of the carrier's mechanics plus two regulators from the Japanese Civil Aviation Bureau. *BOEING*

Pioneering materials and systems characteristics assure the Boeing 787 a place in aerospace history – but, like the Aérospatiale/BAC Concorde in the 1970s, the Dreamliner will also be remembered for its protracted certification.

One positive aspect, however, is that the extra time resulting from the delayed first flight and airworthiness approval enabled Boeing to qualify the 787's claimed large reductions in lifetime maintenance requirements and costs.

As a result, the new twin-aisle twinjet airliner entered service with an unprecedented 12-year interval before (and between) internal structural inspections, which punctuate heavy-maintenance visit (HMV) schedules. This frequency for interior checks of the 787's carbonfibre-reinforced plastic (CFRP) composites structure compares with eight years for the larger 777 and just six years for the smaller 767.

Ironically, having waited an extra three years for the 787's delayed entry into service (EIS), maintenance technicians must now wait a lot longer to look under its skin than if Boeing had kept to its original schedule – which had envisaged a maiden flight in 2007's third quarter being followed by EIS just eight months later in May 2008.

A Dreamliner will first enter an engineering shop, probably in Japan, for an HMV sometime around 2023. Boeing acknowledges that, had the 787 run on time, the company would probably have accepted shorter HMV intervals, as airworthiness authorities had initially requested. Additional time, albeit arising by default, enabled the manufacturer to develop more analytical data to support these longer intervals.

In 2007, after three years of meetings, the 787 maintenance-steering group – comprising airlines, suppliers and airworthiness authorities – recommended intervals for 760 routine systems and structure inspections to

> **FOR THE DREAMLINER, DIGITAL 'TOOLS', GRAPHIC AND TEXTUAL DATABASES REPLACE VOLUMES OF PRINTED PAPER MAINTENANCE DOCUMENTS**

A Rolls-Royce Trent 1000 is manoeuvred into position during an engine change. AIRTEAMIMAGES.COM JORGEN SYVERSEN

A ground crew engineer conducts a visual inspection of a 787 during the aircraft's turnaround. BOEING

the US Federal Aviation Administration and European Aviation Safety Agency: but the regulators rejected 400 of them for lack of analytical data.

In the event, Boeing continued providing information as 787 delays grew, and in December 2008 the two agencies approved all 760 intervals in the maintenance-planning data (MPD) document.

"Approval [followed] the most comprehensive maintenance programme development effort in the history of the industry," claims Boeing. "It [was] supported by more than 33,000 pages of analysis, as well as the participation of eight regulatory agencies, 25 airlines and 30 suppliers and partners."

The company says the 787 maintenance schedule at EIS (including first external inspection after six years and initial 12-year internal checks and landing-gear overhauls) features industry-leading intervals. Basic line, or A check, maintenance is scheduled every 1,000 flight-hours (FH) and base C checks at three years (although Boeing dropped 'letter' checks after the 767, using them now only for model comparison – see table).

Overall, 787 maintenance requirements reflect extensive use of CFRP materials and evolving aircraft systems characteristic of today's new jetliners. Airline engineers and third-party maintenance, repair and overhaul (MRO) providers cite increased application of composites and electrical power as principal considerations in 787 servicing, along with the latest information technology.

For the Dreamliner, digital 'tools', graphic and textual databases replace volumes of printed paper maintenance documents, with Boeing's electronic logbook receiving 787 flight data to share with technicians on the ground.

Previously, they sought repair procedures in hard-copy manuals, but now 787 digitised documents can be obtained on a laptop patented by former 787 chief mechanic Justin Hale. »

Engineers can receive data from the fleet without having to download or retrieve discs. "Maintenance laptops save time and give [faster] access to quality information," says Boeing, the company adding that 787 maintenance comprises longer inspection intervals, reduced inspection time, fewer tasks, less non-routine activity and lower no-fault-found (NFF) rates – the latter at least 50% less than the previous-generation aircraft.

The 787 aircraft health-management (AHM) system gathers vast amounts of maintenance-related data, enabling technicians to 'ask' the aircraft about, for example, tyre pressures, on-board consumption of potable water or levels of galley cooling fluid. Cockpit messages notify system- or part-checks for instant relay to ground terminals, stimulating preparation of replacement parts before the aircraft even lands.

New avionics software is transmitted, installed and tested according to MPD procedures before release for flight. Through centralised fault reporting, the 787 onboard maintenance system (OMS), an "essential tool in maintaining rapid aircraft turnaround rates and maximising despatchability", aids mechanics in isolating faults and guiding maintenance action.

Modern electronics and motors will provide increased overall reliability, decreased costs and improved performance for the Dreamliner, along with reduced weight and parts-count as well as simpler systems installation, says Boeing.

"Overall, mechanical-systems complexity is reduced by more than 50% compared with the 767, providing operators with reduced maintenance costs and improved despatch reliability," the company adds.

The 787's electro-chromatic cabin windows can be controlled with a single command, eliminating 'light-leaking' or inoperable window shades and projecting a life of more than 20 years, according to the manufacturer. Most cabin, flight deck and external illuminations use high-intensity discharge and light-emitting diode (LED) units for dramatically longer lives than incandescent bulbs. Overall, 787 lights will last "ten to 20 times longer" than previous types, with attendant reductions in maintenance replacement.

The OMS, data-load and crew information systems offer 787 operators opportunities to reduce »

OPPOSITE • *The cowlings are open on one of the General Electric GEnx-1B engines that power KLM Royal Dutch Airlines' fleet of Boeing 787-9 Dreamliners.*
LARS VELING

Boeing trains engineers at campuses across the globe. Tools include a 3-D virtual aeroplane, enabling engineers to 'walk' around the aircraft and operate key functions. BOEING

> **MODERN ELECTRONICS AND MOTORS WILL PROVIDE INCREASED OVERALL RELIABILITY, DECREASED COSTS AND IMPROVED PERFORMANCE FOR THE DREAMLINER**

Maintenance **training**

Boeing Training and Flight Services has developed a digital, internet-based 787 maintenance training programme that includes access to a 'virtual' aircraft and systems. Before the Dreamliner's entry into service, the company completed the first course – for ten mechanics from launch customer All Nippon Airways (the first of 150 to be trained over seven months) and two Japan Civil Aviation Bureau regulators.

The course comprises 32 days of theoretical and practical training, engine runs and taxi testing, diagnostic exercises and component identification plus troubleshooting exams, using both the aircraft and a full flight simulator.

One objective is to replicate the whole aircraft to provide performance-based information to technicians in an environment that facilitates practice on the same tools they will use on the real 787.

Students practise using laptop computers to troubleshoot representative situations, with Boeing's maintenance performance 'toolbox solution' providing access to maintenance and fault isolation procedures, parts information and other data.

Component Support

In October 2015, United Airlines announced a ten-year 787 component services contract with Boeing that would set up and maintain a pool of 'rotatable' parts, the manufacturer's third such arrangement following others with Oman Air and British Airways. BA's 12-year deal sees it holding fewer spares while improving component availability.

Similar contracts were established among other 787 operators and maintenance providers, including a $150m Etihad Airways agreement with Abu Dhabi-owned sibling SR Technics, covering component distribution, logistical, technical and engineering support.

European maintenance provider Lufthansa Technik has a ten-year contract with Colombia's Avianca, for which it also supplies 787 production inspection teams at Boeing factories.

An engineer examines and tests an electronic component to ensure it operates safely.
AFI KLM E&M/ PATRICK DELAPIERRE

Boeing Maintenance Schedule Inspection Interval Comparison			
	767	777	787
Line maintenance/A check	750 FH	650 FH	1,000 FH
Base maintenance/C check	6,000 FH/18 months	3 years	6,000 FC/12,000 FH/36 months
External structure/2C check	6,000 FC/3 years	4 years	12,000 FC/6 years
Internal structure/4C check	12,000 FC/6 years	8 years	24,000 FC/12 years
Landing gear overhaul	18,000 FC/10 years	10 years	24,000 FC/12 years
Source: Boeing			

Engineers examine British Airways 787-8, G-ZBJF (c/n 38613), in a hangar at Montreal/Pierre Trudeau International Airport in response to an undisclosed technical issue.
AIRTEAMIMAGES.COM/ MATHIEU POULIOT

A full inspection of a stripped-down General Electric GEnx-1B engine during routine maintenance to identify any signs of any damage.
AFI KLM E&M/ PATRICK DELAPIERRE

OPPOSITE • *Prior to the handover of the first 787 to launch customer All Nippon Airways, Boeing carried out a series of validation flights in Japan enabling both companies to assess the Dreamliner's performance in an operating environment.*
BOEING

maintenance costs, Boeing saying: "Airlines have the option to include a wireless network for maintenance access, enabling 'back-office' teams to remotely deploy software, parts, data, charts and manuals with minimal 'hands-on' mechanic involvement."

The company claims that, at maturity, the 787 will be "guaranteed" 30% less expensive to maintain than comparable aircraft. Systems information and integrated support products will help engineers isolate failed components and reduce return-to-service times.

The 787 uses electrical rather than pneumatic power for engine starts and if the auxiliary power unit (APU) is inoperative, starting can be achieved with external ground power units, says Boeing, which claims that elimination of maintenance-intensive engine bleed-air improves reliability because there are a lot fewer components. Meanwhile the lack of compressed air makes for a simplified and more reliable APU, no-bleed arrangements also offering "significant" maintenance cost and reliability advantages.

Given the 787s single-piece barrel design, fuselage joints are minimised with circumferential splices eliminating the need for longitudinal

lap-joints between overlapping skin panels while reducing weight and drag. The composites fuselage also facilitates non-invasive structural 'crown' inspections without the need to remove any systems or cabin insulation.

With the Dreamliner's maintenance emphasis on electrics replacing most pneumatics while also using fewer parts, overall costs are reduced, says Boeing, which projects labour to be reduced by 20% per check, with total scheduled hours cut by 60% over the life of the aircraft.

The maintenance element of the 787's combined crew information and maintenance system echoes that of the 777. Consolidation of aircraft systems information helps to isolate faults and provides troubleshooting information.

Boeing has introduced wireless local interfaces to both hardware and software – enabling offloading of aircraft data close to a terminal and technicians to exchange maintenance information on and off the aircraft.

A five-year airframe fatigue test completed last year validated the strength of the basic 787 primary structure after simulating 160,000-plus flight cycles – more than 3.6 times the design life (44,000 flight cycles) for the type. Boeing Commercial Airplanes former maintenance engineering director Chris Johnson-Pasqua said all 787 maintenance tasks can be adjusted to match requirements.

Hangar visits are not required until Dreamliners had operated for two years, when a ram-air turbine (RAT) task requires a hydraulic rig and a major power outlet. According to the manufacturer, the MPD accommodates both high-utilisation/short-haul and low-frequency/long-range 787 operations.

Based on fleet performance, Boeing might be able to increase inspection intervals through its statistical analysis scheduled-maintenance optimisation programme.

> **BOEING CLAIMS, AT MATURITY, THAT THE 787 WILL BE "GUARANTEED" 30% LESS EXPENSIVE TO MAINTAIN THAN COMPARABLE AIRCRAFT.**

»

Composites

MAIN • Boeing has ushered in new levels of reliability with the Dreamliner – the use of carbon fibre reinforced plastic composites means there is an unprecedented 12-year interval before (and between) internal inspections.
AIRTEAMIMAGES.COM/ YUKIHIRO KANEKO

Airlines taking delivery of Boeing 787s need to review their capabilities, knowledge, repair processes, materials and training to ensure they are prepared for the type's widespread use of carbonfibre-reinforced plastic composites construction, says the manufacturer.

The Dreamliner structure, which is said to have 30% lower airframe maintenance costs than comparable aircraft, is expected to generate little or no airframe corrosion and fatigue, the two primary drivers for structural repair and maintenance.

As such, 787 maintenance planning data document has no separate corrosion protec-tion and prevention control checks. "Each structural inspection is also for [corrosion] issues," according to Boeing Commercial Airplanes former maintenance engineering director Chris Johnson-Pasqua.

The company set up a sampling pro-gramme with operators, adding: "Based on results of this, the current [structural inspec-tion] intervals will be reviewed."

Given the vulnerability of CFRP composites structures and surfaces to damage from ramp or hangar collisions, Boeing has 'beefed up' accident-prone areas, such as aircraft doors and doorways. Likewise, it has designed the 787 structure to be repaired in the same way as a conventional aluminium-alloy airframe.

"The ability to perform bolted repairs in composites structure is service-proven on the 777 and offers comparable repair times and skills," says the company, which has developed structure repair training courses for operators and MROs.

According to one major repair and overhaul company, "impacts on compos-ites structure elements [can be hard] to identify if no cracks [or] holes are visible. Composites material [reverts] to its original shape after an impact."

All Nippon Airways maintenance engineers being trained on some of the advanced systems incorporated on the Dreamliner.
BOEING

> **"THINK OF THE 787 AS AGEING SLOWER DUE TO A MORE AGE-RESISTANT STRUCTURE.**
>
> **Chris Johnson-Pasqua** Boeing Commercial Airplanes former Maintenance Engineering Director

A technician runs a test on a Boeing 787 auxiliary power unit that has been removed from the aircraft.
AFI KLM E&M/ PATRICK DELAPIERRE

Tasks involving shorter periods include six-year external structural inspections, not requiring removal of many access panels, according to Johnson-Pasqua, who says the most appropriate interval was determined for each task, system and structure: "Airlines are thereby able to package tasks based upon their operating philosophy and policies. The extended intervals also allow greater flexibility."

Although the 787 reaches maturity only after 12 years' service, some "more reliable" systems and structures will not generate higher scheduled maintenance and component failure costs until later, with Boeing saying: "It is Year 24 before 787 costs escalate.

"Think of the 787 as ageing slower due to a more age-resistant structure. After the second [12-year] major inspection, supplemental structural inspections will begin to drive costs up."

Whether airlines maintain their 787s or outsource the work to an MRO is a matter of philosophy. Keeping maintenance in-house provides carriers with ultimate control, but requires operators of mixed fleets to hold a variety of specialist tools or expensive equipment (perhaps limited to use on a single aircraft type) and employ a range of engineering skills.

Conversely, placing business with a third party may lead to less expensive service from a provider enjoying economies of scale from high throughput or specialisation in a single type with related maintenance skills.

With its GoldCare customer service programme, Boeing Commercial Aviation Services and various MRO partners offer operators maintenance and fleet and inventory technical management "at a predictable and competitive cost".

The scheme is also available for 737NG, 747-400, 747-8, and 777 models and offered for the 737 MAX and 777-8 and -9 designs. "More than 60 airlines, covering more than 2,200 aircraft, have performance-based contracts with varying scopes," says Boeing.

The GoldCare programme covers integrated-fleet services and solutions as well as fleet engineering and materials solutions and can be coupled with other, separately available Boeing information systems, including AHM, maintenance performance 'toolbox', electronic flight bag and 'MyBoeingFleet'.

The manufacturer remains confident of its 787 maintenance cost estimates, based on "actual improvements seen when we [have] introduced new aircraft. Past aircraft have not had the key advantages of the 787 structure and systems, so there is a greater step forward than in past new airplanes."

Boeing's Perfect Ten

The Boeing 787-10 is the largest and longest variant of the three-member 787 Dreamliner family. The model was launched during the Paris Air Show in 2013. The initial 787-10 flight test aircraft, N528ZC (c/n 60256), rolled out from Boeing's North Charleston plant in South Carolina, the sole production site for the variant, in January 2017 and undertook its first flight on March 31, 2017.

This jet and two other flight test aircraft, N548ZC (c/n 40929) and N565ZC (c/n 60257), accumulated approximately 900 test hours undertaking the 787-10's flight and certification testing campaign during 2017 to ensure the 787-10 met the manufacturer's internal requirements and US Federal Aviation Administration (FAA) and European Aviation Safety Agency (EASA) certification requirements.

Certification from the FAA was awarded on January 19, 2018, with approval from EASA following on February 28, 2018. The initial customer example, 9V-SCA (c/n 60253), was delivered to launch operator Singapore Airlines (SIA) in March 2018, the airline putting it into service on April 3, 2018. Today there are 98 examples of the 787-10 in use from an order list of 289.

Why the 787-10?

The main aircraft manufacturers offer different aircraft and/or variants of the same type with complementary seating, payload, and range performance to cater for different needs across the widebody, twin-aisle sector.

At the lower end of the widebody market are the Boeing 787-8 and Airbus

Mark Broadbent profiles the Boeing 787-10, the third and latest Dreamliner variant.

A330-800, which with around 250 seats are designed to cater for airlines' lower-capacity and market-opening requirements. The 787-9 and A330-900 sit in the 250–300 seats segment of the market, with the 777/777X and A350-1000 optimised for 350-plus seats.

The 787-10 sits between the 787-9/A330-900 and the 777/A350-1000 in the segment for 300 to 350 seats. Its primary head-to-head competitor is the A350-900. The 787-10 is optimised to carry 330 seats in a typical two-class layout (32 in business class and 298 in economy) or up to a maximum of 440 seats in a single-class configuration. Its revenue cargo capacity is 6,722ft3 and the aircraft can operate routes of up to 6,430nm range.

The 787-10 cannot fly as far as its Dreamliner stablemates: the 787-8's typical range is 7,355nm and the 787-9's is 7,635nm. The 787-10 was expressly designed to offer airlines the ability to put more capacity on medium to long-haul range routes where demand characteristics justify it.

Larger in size also means the 787-10 carries more revenue cargo.

According to Boeing's latest Airplane Characteristics for Airport Planning document, the 787-10's underfloor cargo volume provides space for 22 LD-3 containers (each sized at 158ft3) in the forward compartment and 18 in the aft compartment. This total of 40 LD-3s is four more than the 787-9 and 12 more than the 787-8. There is also 402ft3 volume in the bulk cargo compartment. Total cargo capacity is 15% more than the 787-9 and 41% more than the 787-8.

What is Different?

A longer fuselage is the most obvious difference between the 787-10 and its 787-8 and 787-9 stablemates. At 224ft in total length, the 787-10 is 18ft longer than the 206ft 787-9 and 38ft longer than the 186ft 787-8. All the Dreamliner variants share the same 197ft wingspan, 56ft height and 18ft 11in fuselage cross-section.

The 787-10 is technically a 'double stretch' of the 787-9; Boeing took the 787-9's fuselage and added five frames forward of the wing (which make up 10ft of the 18ft extra length) and four frames aft of the wing (which make up the other 8ft).

The variant has a maximum take-off weight of 560,000lb, the same as the 787-9. However, a longer fuselage creates more surface area and therefore higher structural loads, necessitating local strengthening on certain areas of the lower empennage.

The extra length also results in a crucial difference between the 787-10 and the other variants: a semi-levered landing gear. The 787-10's main landing gear truck has an additional actuator that locks out and means the pivot point around which the aircraft rotates on take-off is different. The 787-10's pivot point is around the aft wheel of the landing gear truck rather than the midpoint, as on the other Dreamliners.

Changing any part of the structure on an aircraft for a new variant obviously changes the parent model's handling characteristics, so Boeing had to adjust the Dreamliner's fly-by-wire flight control system (FCS) control laws accordingly.

The 787-10 features a specific control law that if it detects a potential tail strike it commands the elevators to generate nose-down pitch to adjust the fuselage's attitude, which increases the clearance between the fuselage and the runway and the safety margin for rotation and flare.

A priority in flight testing the variant was assessing the longer fuselage's impact on the aircraft's handling and control. Take-off and landing performance tests were conducted at Edwards Air Force Base in California, and crosswind landing trials took place at Gander International Airport in Newfoundland, Canada to validate the variant's performance. »

KLM's first 787-10 PH-BKA (c/n 42485) arrives in Amsterdam in June 2019. KLM ROYAL DUTCH AIRLINES/ PAUL RIDDERHOF

Vertical Modal Suppression

Another significant difference between the 787-10 and the other Dreamliners is a flaps up vertical modal suppression system or FoVMS.

As explained in an FAA document published on the US Federal Register detailing the special-condition justification from Boeing for the FoVMS, the 787-10's longer fuselage degraded the flutter performance of the Dreamliner wing, nacelle, and body.

The traditional ways of dampening flutter to an acceptable margin are either to increase the torsional stiffness of the wing or add ballast weights into the design of the wingtips. The FAA wrote in its document that Boeing rejected these options because it felt they, "do not meet [the company's] business objectives." Instead, the company proposed introducing a new control law for the normal mode of the 787-10's primary FCS to satisfy the flutter-damping margin requirements.

The paper explained: "The FoVMS system will be active in certain parts of the flight envelope when the flaps are retracted. The FoVMS system is a feedback-control system that adds damping to the system's 3Hz mode by oscillating the elevators symmetrically. When the elevators are expected to be ineffective due to blowdown or other limitations, the flaperons are applied to augment or supplant elevator-control input."

A further important difference between the 787-10 and its Dreamliner stablemates is the larger, longer variant's more powerful engines: either General Electric (GE) GEnx-1B76s or Rolls-Royce Trent 1000 TEN (Thrust, Efficiency, New technology) turbofans.

According to the manufacturers' datasheets, the GEnx-1B76 variant on the 787-10 provides 76,100lb (338kN) take-off thrust and the Trent 1000 TEN generates 78,000lb (347kN) take-off thrust compared to the 74,100lb-thrust (329kN) GEnx/Trent 1000 variants on the 787-9 and the 69,800lb (310kN) variants on the 787-8.

The Trent 1000 TEN uses technologies from the Trent XWB engine developed for the A350, specifically a scaled-down intermediate pressure and high-pressure (HP) compressor first developed for the Trent XWB-84 powering the A350-900 and the HP turbine architecture first developed for the A350-1000's Trent XWB-97.

Other differences between the Trent 1000 TEN and the latest Trent 1000 Package C engines on the 787-8 and 787-9 are a modulated air system, an increased use of composites, redesigned external systems, a new external gearbox, and an updated

The Boeing 787-10 features a semi-levered landing gear that means the pivot point around which the aircraft rotates on take-off is different from 787-8 and 787-9. BOEING

engine control system. Rolls-Royce says the Trent 1000 TEN provides a 2% fuel burn improvement compared to earlier Trent 1000s.

Materials Used

Although the 787-10 features more powerful engines, the FoVMS, the semi-levered landing gear and the additional FCS control law, the differences between the aircraft and the other Dreamliner variants are minimal and deliberately so, because structural and systems commonality means operators can retain the same procedures for maintenance and crew training and common spares holdings. Boeing says there is over 95% commonality in part numbers between the 'Dash Ten' and the other Dreamliners.

As per the other 787 variants, advanced materials make up more than 65% of the 787-10's structure by weight, with carbon fibre composites accounting for nearly 50% and titanium for 15%. Other materials in the aircraft include aluminium or aluminium lithium (20%) and steel (10%).

Carbon laminate structures, produced by forming carbon fibre infused with a resin into a tape before lamination, are used in the fuselage, vertical and horizontal stabilisers, wing covers and wing leading edges. There are carbon sandwich structures, produced by attaching two thin but stiff skins to a lightweight core, in the vertical and horizontal stabilisers and wings.

Electrical System

Along with the extensive use of advanced materials, another key feature in the 787 Dreamliner is its electrical architecture.

The traditional method of powering secondary systems is to divert bleed air from the engines to generators and the auxiliary power unit (APU) for pneumatic power. Although it is incorrect to say the 787 is totally bleedless, as bleed air is still used for certain functions such as some anti-ice systems and pressurising hydraulic reservoirs, most of the functions that usually rely on bleed air on the Dreamliner are driven instead by electrical power.

Boeing says the architecture reduces maintenance costs and improves engine efficiency, because the 787 does not feature extensive pneumatic components such as ducts, valves, heat shields, starters, and compressors. On the Dreamliner, generators on each engine and the APU are directly connected to the engine gearboxes that drive electric motors that distribute power to the aircraft's electrical/ electronics (E/E) bay and remote power distribution units (RPDUs).　　　》

After evaluating an enhanced version of the high-pressure turbine fan blade for the Trent 1000 TEN, Rolls-Royce introduced the enhanced blade in 2020. *ROLLS-ROYCE*

The Boeing 787-10, the third and largest Dreamliner variant, launched in 2013, completed its first flight in 2017 and entered service in 2018. *BOEING*

The 787-10's flight deck is dominated by large-format LCD screens. This is the cockpit of a United Airlines aircraft.
AIRTEAMIMAGES/4X6ZK-MONI SHAFIR

Boeing has sold fewer than 300 examples of the 787-10 since launching the variant in 2013. BOEING

Air New Zealand has ordered eight 787-10s to replace its 777-200ERs. AIR NEW ZEALAND

In turn, the functionality of critical systems on the 787 is different from other aircraft. To give some examples, the converters used for engine and APU start, and the hydraulic pumps used to support flight controls, landing gear, thrust reversers and control surfaces are driven by electric motors. On the 787, wing anti-ice protection, traditionally provided by discharging hot bleed air into the wing through a valve, is provided by the electrical system energising heating blankets bonded to the interior of the protected slat leading edges, while the Dreamliner's brakes are electrically rather than hydraulically actuated.

Electrical actuation enabled Boeing to eliminate physical circuit breakers in the flight deck. According to the manufacturer, 13 line replaceable units are needed to provide the full complement of flight deck display, communication, navigation, and surveillance equipment.

Boeing had nothing drastic to change on the established architecture despite the 787-10's larger size, the work being to tune up the system to meet the extra power demands by using the inherent margin designed into the system to uprate the capability of the generators, E/E bays, RPDUs, and the wiring.

The electrical system also contributes to one of the key differences about the 787, one the manufacturer and airlines like to emphasise: the feel of the cabin. The environmental control system controlling air conditioning and pressurisation uses electrically driven, adjustable-speed motor compressors, which compress air (drawn aboard from outside the aircraft via inlets) through low-pressure air-conditioning packs.

Another major design feature of the 787 is its battery system comprising two primary rechargeable lithium-ion batteries: an APU battery housed just behind the wings in the aft E/E bay and a main battery in the forward E/E bay.

The 787-10 of course has the features – including insulators around each battery cell, wire sleeving and upgraded wiring, fasteners, stainless steel enclosures and venting systems – introduced to the Dreamliner as fixes for the battery issues that caused incidents in early 2013 on Japan Airlines and All Nippon Airlines 787s and grounded Dreamliners for months. »

Flight Deck

The Boeing 787 Dreamliner flight deck was designed to be both innovative and offer extensive commonality in layout and operating procedures with previous Boeing flight decks, especially the 777. This enabled the manufacturer to pursue a common type rating between the two and minimise training time.

Boeing retained its wheel-and-column control layout, and the FCS uses some of the 777's flight control laws, the aircraft exhibiting similar handling characteristics. Cockpit displays, switches and controls were deliberately positioned like a 777's, and pre-flight procedures and checklists are similar.

Boeing says the commonality means pilots already qualified on the 777 can transition on to the 787 in as little as five days. Pilots with no experience in a Boeing flight deck will need 21 days of training, the company says.

The 787-10's cockpit includes five multifunction displays (MFDs), dual head-up displays (HUDs) and the dual electronic flight bags (EFBs). The MFD screens are Collins Aerospace liquid crystal displays which diagonally measure 15.1in.

The two outboard MFDs show primary flight display information combined with an auxiliary display consolidating frequently referenced information such as the flight number, radio frequencies and the aircraft transponder code. The lower portion of the auxiliary display shows datalink messages, controller-pilot datalink communications, and digital automated terminal information.

The MFDs can be split into independent formats or configured to provide a single large navigation map. Pilots can select other MFD formats, including synoptic displays showing data for major systems, electronic checklist (ECL), and an electronic control display unit interface. Pilots can also tailor how they want the MFDs to present information.

Honeywell's triple-redundant flight management system (FMS) supplies all navigation, maintenance and crew information systems, electronics, and FCS on the aircraft.

Among the systems to aid crew situational awareness are integrated approach navigation, an enhanced vertical situational display (which provides a graphic rendering of approaching terrain and a picture of the FMS-calculated vertical flight profile), a ground moving map, integrated surveillance systems providing weather radar, transponder, a traffic collision avoidance system, and ground proximity functionality. There is redundancy to support automatic dependent surveillance-broadcast and dual HUDs showing the pilots the standard information needed to fly the aircraft.

The Dreamliner was initially certified to operate up to 180 minutes' flying time away from a landing site, but additional extended-range operations capabilities allow 787s to be operated up to 330 minutes flying time away.

Several 787 operators that the author spoke with in recent years, such as Virgin Atlantic and TUI, cited the ECL as a particularly useful feature of the flight deck. The ECL is useful not just for replacing paper checklists, but also in minimising the omission of checklist items. This is because some items in the ECL are closed loop, which means the system automatically checks if a switch or lever is in the proper position. This means pilots can't leave anything out, the ECL notifying the pilots if there is an issue that requires attention.

The 787 has dual Class 3 touchscreen EFB compatibility. A further benefit of the flight deck's design is accessing information from the FMS using the EFBs. An onboard performance tool (OPT) enables flight and maintenance crews to conduct real-time calculations based on current weather and runway conditions to calculate the take-off and landing numbers and weight and balance information. The system corrects for pressure variations, runway conditions, engine bleeds and minimum equipment list variations.

Rather than performing calculations using manuals, the crew enters all the information about the take-off and landing, take-off weights and fuel weights and weather data into the system, with the OPT then generating optimal thrust rating and flap settings for the crew to use. Moreover, the system will tell pilots if there's an error, for example if erroneous weight information is entered.

The dual HUDs of course provide pilots with flight information in their line of sight. Autothrottle capability and asymmetry compensation through the flight controls means engine-out handling is straightforward for the pilots.

How Airlines Use the 787-10

The 787-10 provides a replacement for ageing, medium to long-haul aircraft configured with 300 to 350 seats, namely the legacy A330 variants and the 777-200ER. Boeing says the aircraft provides superior operating costs: 25% less fuel per seat than those aircraft, as well as 10% less than the current competition (principally the A350-900).

Air New Zealand told the author the 787-10's performance was 'fundamental' to its evaluation process and its eventual decision to order eight examples to replace its 777-200ERs and join its 787-9s. The airline said: "We've chosen the 787-10 for its unrivalled fuel efficiency and carbon saving benefits."

As part of its June 18, 2021, investor update, Air New Zealand announced it had recently negotiated with Boeing to delay the delivery date of its first 787-10 from 2023 to 2024. The decision driven by the COVID-19 pandemic's impact on international air travel.

Most 787-10 customers are of course the large network airlines such as United, SIA and British Airways who already operate the 787-8 and/or 787-9 and for these carriers the largest Dreamliner gives extra capacity to core markets with large demand so they can maximise revenues.

The largest carriers also value the ability to move aircraft around their network to account for changing patterns in passenger demand, right-sizing for each route. For example, if a route begun with a smaller-capacity 787-8 saw increased demand from passengers, an operator can switch the smaller variant for a 787-10 to capture the higher demand. Alternatively, if demand dropped, an airline could instead substitute the larger variant for the smaller jet to serve the route, enabling the operator to keep the service, but do so more cost-effectively, therefore freeing-up the 'Ten' to do something else.

Sales Prospects

When the 787-10 was launched in 2013, Steven Udvar-Hazy, the chief executive of the Air Lease Corporation, which had placed an order for 30 787-10s, commended the variant's "ideal size, capabilities and economical operating costs."

However, since the jet's launch, Boeing has attracted just 289 orders for the variant. Although many factors influence aircraft purchasing – airlines' future fleet planning and the timescales for these requirements, production availability, commonality with existing aircraft, wider macroeconomics influencing market conditions and fuel price – a figure of less than a couple of hundred orders in more than six years is a slow take-up, and it is a figure some way down on the variant's head-to-head competitor, the A350-900, which by May 2025 had amassed over 1000 orders. ✈

Commonality between the larger 787-10 and its Dreamliner stablemates is a key selling point of the variant. Korean Air has made a strong commitment to the 787, with 21 currently in operation and another 40 on order, including 20 ordered at the 2024 Farnborough Air Show. *BOEING*

EVA Air took delivery of its first 787-10 in June 2019. *BOEING*

Launch customer All Nippon Airways (ANA) chose this special livery for the first two Boeing 787 Dreamliners it received, JA801A (c/n 34488) and JA802A (c/n 34497). The carrier reverted to its standard livery, albeit with '787' titles on the forward fuselage, for later deliveries.
AIRTEAMIMAGES.COM/ YUKIHIRO KANEKO

Air New Zealand was the launch customer for the stretched 787-9. The national carrier painted its initial example, ZK-NZE (c/n 34334), in an eye-catching overall black livery.
AIRTEAMIMAGES.COM/ EDWIN CHAI

Japan Airlines Boeing 787-8, JA828J (c/n 34838), wore 'Sora wo Tobu' (Flying Sky) decals on its fuselage for a short period as part of a collaboration with Japanese animation film company, Studio Ghibli. The aircraft was returned to its standard livery.
AIRTEAMIMAGES.COM/ YUKIHIRO KANEKO

China Southern Airlines adopted this special livery for its new Boeing 787 fleet. Here, B-2732 (c/n 34926), is captured on final approach to London/Heathrow in September 2013.
AIRTEAMIMAGES.COM/ STEVE FLINT

One of the most spectacular Dreamliner schemes to date must surely be All Nippon Airways 787-9, JA873A (c/n 34530), which was painted in R2-D2-inspired livery to promote the Star Wars film: The Force Awakens.
SETH JAWORSKI

Chinese carrier Hainan Airlines wears one of the brightest liveries of any Dreamliner. The airline ordered ten 787-8s with the final example, B-2759 (c/n 38056) joining its fleet in March 2015. *AIRTEAMIMAGES. COM/ 4X6ZK-MONI SHAFIR*

Boeing Business Jets has sold VIP versions of both current variants of the Dreamliner – the BBJ 787-8 and BBJ 787-9. One such example, A6-PFC (c/n 35303), is operated by the Abu Dhabi Amiri Flight on behalf of the Government of the UAE.
RAINER BEXTEN

Budget carrier Scoot painted Boeing 787-9, 9V-OJE (c/n 37116), in this striking livery as part of Singapore's Golden Jubilee celebrations in 2015.
AIRTEAMIMAGES.COM/ THOMAS K

A Troupe of Production
ISSUES

Mark Ayton provides insight to the production issues currently impacting Boeing's 787 programme.

On September 7, 2020, *The Wall Street Journal* reported that Boeing had informed the Federal Aviation Administration (FAA) that sections of the aft fuselage produced for the 787 at its North Charleston facilities failed to meet its own design and manufacturing standards. The report was based on an internal August 31, 2020 FAA memo seen by the newspaper. According to the memo, at the time an FAA review was considering mandating accelerated inspections of hundreds of 787s.

Shims are used to fill gaps during the assembly process. Some shims within the aft body section of a batch of aircraft produced in early 2019 were found to be incorrectly sized. That process involved the use of ultrasound scanners and tools able to measure the small out-of-tolerance gaps. Boeing says there was no safety of flight issue, and the problem was corrected.

According to a Boeing spokeswoman this was a specific issue related to software measurement. She said: "There was no need for rework or anything else related to the fleet with the initial finding."

Over 1,000 Dreamliner aircraft currently flying are thought to have out-of-tolerance gaps.

This was the first of many issues discovered on the 787 Dreamliner.

Composite Skin Flatness

In August 2020, Boeing identified a second issue – composite skin flatness - in the same area of the aft body caused by software failing to flag shims which exceeded the maximum thickness as per the specifications.

Once Boeing had identified skin flatness in the aft carbon composite body sections, it adopted a proactive approach to look across the entire fuselage to determine if there were similar composite skin flatness issues elsewhere. Suppliers were instructed to assess production of the fuselage sections at their facilities to determine whether similar conditions were present – some were found.

Boeing and its suppliers found more areas where the skin flatness did not meet the standard.

Describing the issue, Boeing said: "Slight waviness in the composite skin at the joint areas was not as flush as it needed to be but was not an immediate safety of flight issue."

*ABOVE • **A Boeing 787-10 in assembly at Boeing's North Charleston plant.** BOEING*

Chronology of Events

Date	Issue
August 2019	Shims used in assembly were found to be an incorrect size.
September 2020	Skin-flatness related to gaps in aft-body fuselage sections at the joins exceeded the design specification.
November 2020	Deliveries halted.
March 2021	Boeing's inspection authority removed by the FAA.
March 2021	Deliveries resumed.
May 2021	Deliveries suspended.
July 2021	Production cut to five aircraft per month.
July 2021	Issues with the forward pressure bulkhead on certain un-delivered 787s were discovered.
September 2021	Fixes for some of 48 production issues were overdue to the FAA.
October 2021	Some titanium parts made by a supplier were produced with the wrong alloy.
November 2021	Contamination of composite material used in structural parts was discovered.
November 2021	Gaps in the structures surrounding aft passenger and cargo doors on some in-production 787s caused by waviness in the composite skin material at joins discovered.
January 2022	Costs attributed to the 787 issues announced in Boeing's Q4 CY2021 results were US$4.54bn.

Boeing operates a notice of escapement (NOE) process in which a supplier provides written notification to Boeing when a non-conformance is determined to exist, or is suspected to exist, on a product already delivered to Boeing. Self-reporting of an openness about issues that arise is an expectation held by Boeing and its suppliers.

A Boeing spokesperson said: "We're seeing a series of NOEs for which a produced part or assembly doesn't match the intended engineering standard. An NOE is part of the overall process of how we deal with areas of production that don't match the intended design. By using engineering analysis, Boeing engineers can assess if a specific NOE is a safety of flight issue and which action is required: inspection, replacement, modification, or continued usage as is."

Grounding

However, with the two issues located in the same area Boeing undertook engineering analysis and determined the combination of the two — shims and a non-flat inner skin surface — could create unacceptable gaps. Consequently, eight aircraft had to be grounded for rework before returning into service. The in-service 787 fleet continued and continues to operate normally. A Boeing spokeswoman told the author the company is continuing to work through the process to determine whether there is an action

Composite materials make up 50% of the primary structure of the 787 Dreamliner, including the fuselage and wing. According to a feature published by The Seattle Times based on facts in an FAA memo, by November 2021 Boeing was faced with a contamination issue with carbon-fibre composite material used in the fabrication of the large structures used for 787 wings and fuselage sections.
BOEING

for the in-service fleet, and that they have 110 aircraft awaiting rework.

According to a Boeing spokesperson, the company has followed its quality assessment process throughout. Once a potential problem is identified, Boeing engineers determine whether the issue has occurred at other locations and if that might be problematic. This is undertaken to ensure the aircraft meets its design specification.

A Troupe of Issues

On October 14, 2021, *The Wall Street Journal* published details of an FAA letter sent on September 6 and which had been seen by its editorial staff. The letter prompted Boeing to improve or fix 48 non-compliant production processes to federal standards. The newspaper reported that more than a quarter of the items cited in the FAA letter had been solved by mid-October.

When asked for some examples and what actions Boeing had taken to improve, the Boeing spokeswoman declined to provide details.

In mid-March 2021, FAA air-safety regulators stripped Boeing's authority to inspect and sign off on newly produced 787 Dreamliner aircraft, a status still in effect today. This means that FAA inspectors perform the pre-delivery safety checks required to issue airworthiness certificates for customer handover.

By July, Boeing had discovered an issue with the forward pressure »

bulkhead on certain 787s among the 100-plus undelivered aircraft with a market value over US$25bn.

In early October, the type's situation had not improved when the framer announced that titanium parts used on some 787s built since 2018 are weaker than required.

A memo between the FAA and Boeing that had been seen by *The Seattle Times* identified the most critical installation as the floor-beam-to-fuselage-frame fittings at the side of body area where the wings attach. In the memo, the FAA stated the issue could present an unsafe condition if two or more adjacent fittings are made of the wrong titanium alloy. More than 450 787s are affected.

On November 19, 2021, *The Seattle Times* published a feature based on facts in an FAA memo that detailed yet another defect: contamination of carbon-fibre composite material. The newspaper said Boeing had informed the FAA how Japan's Mitsubishi Heavy Industries discovered contamination of the composite material during fabrication of the large structures used for wings, fuselage sections and tails of the 787. The contamination with Teflon residue reportedly reduces the strength of joins between composite parts bonded with adhesives. The Teflon residue was released from bagging used in the production process making the composite structure non-compliant with Boeing's manufacturing specification.

A Boeing spokeswoman said the company had assessed potential contamination across the production

In late November 2014, Boeing started final assembly of the 787-9 Dreamliner at its North Charleston, South Carolina facility. The plant now produces all variants of the 787 Dreamliner following consolidation from the original Everett, Washington plant in July 2021. BOEING

system to determine if Teflon is the cause, and whether it has an impact on the aircraft's structure, but it's not a 787-specific issue.

At the same mid-November timeframe, FlightGlobal reported on a confirmation from Boeing that its programme of rework on structures surrounding aft passenger and cargo doors on some in-production 787s was nearing completion.

According to an FAA memo seen by *The Seattle Times* the issue with structures surrounding aft passenger and cargo doors was caused by gaps in the structure resulting from waviness in the composite skin material at joins. The FAA memo listed imprecision of robotic equipment used to fabricate the structures.

When asked how efforts to improve production as initiated by Boeing's CEO, David Calhoun were going, a Boeing spokeswoman said: "We're taking a proactive approach to improve quality and meet all standards, which requires a significant amount of labour. We haven't put a timeline on it. We're working closely with the FAA throughout to share information with them as we've assessed the various areas on the fuselage. Through continued engineering assessment, continued rework in our factories in North Charleston and Everett, we're preparing to resume delivery once we've met the standard required by the FAA."

Quality control problems led to production delays and stoppages and a cessation in deliveries between

November 2020 and August 2022. In early 2023, deliveries were delayed once again when data analysis issues were identified.

In June 2024, Reuters reported that Boeing was investigating issues arising from incorrect installation of fasteners on fuselages. The company did not envisage impact on deliveries.

As of spring 2025, deliveries have resumed with a current production rate of five per month, which the company hopes to raise to seven per month by the end of the year.

At the time of going to press, it remains to be seen how production and certification of the 787 will be affected by the tragic loss of Air India Flight 171 (VT-ANB, serial 36279), in June 2025. This was the first fatal incident involving a Dreamliner

Higher Gross Weight

The author asked Boeing for detail of higher gross weight versions of the 787-9 and 787-10 as broken by *The Seattle Times*. A spokesman provided the following statement: "We are developing an increased maximum take-off weight plan for the 787-9 and 787-10 that will add additional value for our customers with even greater efficiency, flexibility, and capability. The 787's unique combination of those attributes has made it a preferred aircraft for both airlines and passengers. We are always having conversations with our customers to see how we can provide them more value and help them operate more efficiently."

No details about payload and range gains were available.